CW00481917

SAINT WITH THE
SILVER SHOES

The Continuing Search for St Walstan

Carol Twinch

A S S O C I A T E S

By the same author:

So You Want to Keep Sheep
Plain and Simple Egg Production
Poultry: a Guide to Management
Women on the Land: Their Story During Two World Wars
In Search of St Walstan: East Anglia's Enduring Legend
Tithe War 1918-1939: The Countryside in Revolt
Great Suffolk Stories

FIRST EDITION 2004

Published by Media Associates, Norwich, Norfolk
Front cover The Boardroom Design Studio
Printed and bound by The Lavenham Press, Lavenham, Suffolk
Distributed by GLF Books, PO Box 36, Saxmundham, Suffolk IP17 2PS
GLFBooks@hotmail.com

All rights reserved
No part of this book may be reproduced by any means
without the prior written permission of the author

© Carol Twinch 2004

ISBN 0 9521499 3 1

CONTENTS

Photographs from the author's collection unless otherwise stated

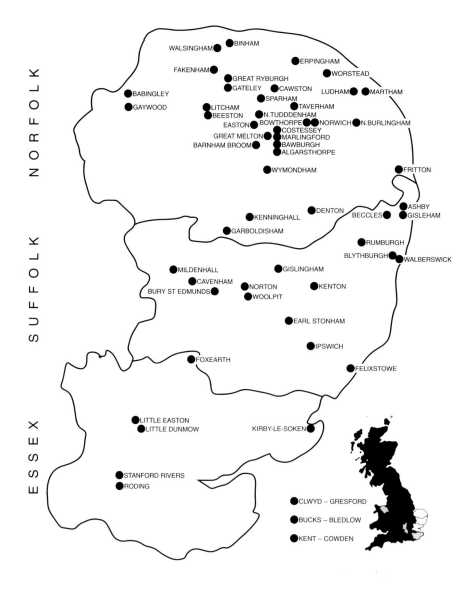

NORFOLK

SUFFOLK

ESSEX

WALSINGHAM ●
● BINHAM
● ERPINGHAM
FAKENHAM ●
● WORSTEAD
● GREAT RYBURGH
● GATELEY   ● CAWSTON
LUDHAM ● ● MARTHAM
● SPARHAM
● BABINGLEY
● TAVERHAM
● GAYWOOD
● LITCHAM
● N.TUDDDENHAM
● BEESTON
EASTON ● ● BOWTHORPE ● NORWICH ● N.BURLINGHAM
● COSTESSEY
GREAT MELTON ● ● MARLINGFORD
BARNHAM BROOM ● ● BAWBURGH
● ALGARSTHORPE
● WYMONDHAM
● FRITTON
● DENTON
● ASHBY
● KENNINGHALL
BECCLES ● ● GISLEHAM
● GARBOLDISHAM
● RUMBURGH
BLYTHBURGH ●
● WALBERSWICK
● MILDENHALL
● GISLINGHAM
● CAVENHAM
BURY ST EDMUNDS ● ● NORTON
● KENTON
● WOOLPIT
● EARL STONHAM
● IPSWICH
● FOXEARTH
● FELIXSTOWE
● LITTLE EASTON
● LITTLE DUNMOW
KIRBY-LE-SOKEN ●
● STANFORD RIVERS
● RODING
● CLWYD – GRESFORD
● BUCKS – BLEDLOW
● KENT – COWDEN

INTRODUCTION

HARDLY WAS THE INK of *In Search of St Walstan* dry than a letter arrived to say that Gateley had been left out of the gazetteer. Then hot on its heels came the forgotten reredos at St Laurence's in Norwich, plus a secular, 20th-century glass panel of SS Walstan and Felix in Costessey. Yet more omissions – a fine 20th-century window containing St Walstan at Stanford Rivers in Essex and another at Kirby-le-Soken – made a second volume inevitable. Then came discoveries via the internet of modern windows in Kent and Buckinghamshire and, at the eleventh hour, just a few weeks before publication came a telephone call from Dr John Blatchly, to say that he had identified St Walstan in flint flushwork on at least two Norfolk churches.

Once the newly transcribed will bequests began to show that men and women were making pilgrimages to St Walstan's Well from all over East Anglia, the destruction in 1999 of the pilgrim's lane – which led from the church to St Walstan's Well – was made all the more poignant. Memories were stirred of the Bishop's Pilgrimage when some 450 pilgrims, led by Bishop Peter, approached the church of St Mary & St Walstan from Algarsthorpe and joined the path down to the well, as so many had done before them over hundreds of years. The beautiful, hollowed-out lane which edged the south-west corner of the churchyard, with its unique sloping banks, exists now only in the memory of those who saw it before the bulldozers did their work.

In 1995, Charles Roberts wrote of the procession at that year's Patronal Service:

Under a shifting sky of sunlight shafts and gathering cloud a procession wends its way down a country track between frothing banks of cow parsley. Above them on its knoll, around which the track curves, the ancient round tower of the village church, old as Ethelred and topped by its eccentric candle-snuffer cap, glints flintily.

A small boy led the procession down from the church into the roughly scythed clearing between the trees and to the site of St Walstan's Well:

This is history and heritage … heritage in action, perpetuating a gentle tradition which goes back nearly 1000 years.

Is there hope that over the next thousand years the footsteps of pilgrims will re-dedicate the lane, simply by using it, reinforcing the faint echo of ancient feet and wearing down the tarmac until the earth dips again? That decision lies with successive generations; like church buildings and other sacred sites, the continuance of St Walstan at Bawburgh will only survive if people want it to.

Moments of compensatory magic in this new search for St Walstan include sitting in the hallowed portals of the Bodleian's Duke Humfrey's Library in Oxford, with its sepulchral avenues of dimly lit reading benches, holding the small 14th-century psalter and seeing St Walstan's name inscribed in it. Then hearing about the window at Beccles, followed closely by the revelations from Peter Northeast about St Walstan's silver shoes. Trying to overcome initial scepticism at the Garboldisham flints, it was doubly exciting to discover the 1506 will of John atte Cherche, which proved local knowledge of St Walstan and thus made the crowned Ws at Erpingham, Fakenham and Garboldisham a definite possibility.

Interestingly, St Sidwell turns out to have more in common with St Walstan than just their scythes. In *The Voices of Morebath*, Eamon Duffy (who brought St Walstan to prominence in the ground-breaking *Stripping of the Altars*) recounts the story of St Sidwell's silver shoe. In 1529 a woman parishioner bequeathed her silver wedding ring to St Sidwell that it should be melted down to make her a shoe. In Morebath, as at Bawburgh, the need for a local saint was satisfied by claiming one for its own and when, in 1538, Henry VIII's reformers set about the destruction of the shrines there were, no doubt, churchwardens and parishioners in more places than Morebath and Bawburgh who rescued and hid relics of much-loved saints.

It is to be hoped that St Walstan's silver shoes did not suffer the fate of the one made for St Sidwell, which was stolen from her shrine in 1534 by a thief who broke into the church and made off with the chalice and the silver shoe. Perhaps Walstan's were painted onto his image and so more difficult to steal: thus might the silver shoes and pennies have survived until at least 1538. It would, after all, be less expensive to have painted shoes than solid silver shoes, and the wording of Robert Clarke's will indicates 'painting' of the image.

SS Walstan and Sidwell are but two of a myriad of such shrines dotted across medieval Europe, but they serve as perfect examples of local saints becoming the very heart of the communities in which they were revered (although at Bawburgh the Shrine Chapel was a satellite of the Norwich Priory while devotion at Morebath was more a parish matter). Professor Eamon Duffy has done a fine job of exploring what the word 'Reformation' hides and what it meant at parish level, especially in the countryside, where rural tradition is engrained in the culture and lives of everyone concerned.

The story of the English Life continues to intrigue and mystify. Several questions about its origins were posed in *In Search of St Walstan*, in particular what connections Archdeacon Philip Tenison had with Bawburgh. However, during research into the life of Archbishop Thomas Tenison and the origins of Queen Anne's Bounty, it emerged that Philip Tenison had not only lived in Bawburgh but had a school there. Edward Carpenter wrote:

> *Owing to this persecution of the Episcopal clergy, [Philip Tenison] set up a school at Bawburgh in Norwich, where he remained until he was appointed to the Rectory of Foulsham at the Restoration, and was made Archdeacon of Norfolk the same year.*

This opened up all kinds of imaginings, some of them contained in Chapter 2, but the English Life retains its secret and we are still unable to draw any better or firmer conclusions.

But, just as dendrochronology is helping to uncover the origins of wood in the fabric and furniture of pre-Reformation churches, so new technology will prise out secrets from ancient documents and, were the will and the funding made available, the Scribe's name could be among them. In 2003 the Fitzwilliam Museum in Cambridge unveiled new methods of revealing underlying details in manuscripts that cannot otherwise be seen. Intricate photography (developed by Océ, specialists in document-management technology) was used for the digitisation of a 1460s prayer book that revealed hidden images and details known only to the original artist and impossible to see with the naked eye.

The news of a Walstan window at Bledlow took the search to a particularly wonderful corner of Buckinghamshire. Thanks to a programme of reintroduction the gregarious Red Kites now circle and soar, their six-foot wingspan an awesome sight as they ride the wind, mewing plaintively as they gather in their hundreds above the Chilterns. In medieval times Kites scavenged for carrion on the streets of towns and villages and, though wild, are not afraid to sweep down into the valleys to feed. The fabric of the Holy Trinity has benefited from its glorious setting, which was used in the television series *Midsomer Murders*, and the St Walstan window looks just right in rural Buckinghamshire.

Cowden, on the Kent/Sussex border, is not unlike Bledlow in that it is a picturesque English village with beautifully kept houses and an immaculate church. This is a modern window, but did a 15th-century Kentish pilgrim really forsake St Thomas of Canterbury for St Walstan and did he then evangelise the story of East Anglia's farming saint in Kent? The pilgrim is not named but the miracle of the Curing of the Canterbury Weaver by St Walstan is the longest of the eleven miracles of the English Life, indicating the importance to the Bawburgh shrine-keepers of a link with the more famous St Thomas.

Yet such ponderings are surely nothing more than sentimental and romantic, a fanciful 'stamp collecting' form of historical research rather than serious, academic study? Indeed, many such ponderings will undoubtedly slip into this book, but then it is not intended as an academic treatise. Rather it aims to bring together all aspects of the thousand year-old story, see how it survived into the 21st century and raise a few unanswered questions. What became of St Walstan's silver shoes … what really happened on 29 September 1658 … how did the triptych remain hidden for 120 years … and was the Life of St Walstan the figment of someone's imagination?

Amateur enthusiasm is endearing to some and annoying to others, but this is no apology for continuing to leave no stone unturned in the search for St Walstan. It is my contention that more discoveries will be made which will further illuminate the cult and legend of St Walstan, and, while he could not be numbered among the great saints of pre-Reformation Christianity, his following united souls across at least three counties. The suggestion of the crowned letter W on church towers standing for St Walstan is likely to be considered more seriously in the light of a proven extent for the cult. Could he have been what we might now call The People's Saint, rather than one championed by the great and powerful? It is puzzling that so few saints appear to represent the ordinary men and women of the primary occupation, farming. Maybe he was honoured more by ordinary men and women, as evidenced by their wills, and was so well known in rural parishes that the craftsman at Garboldisham was able to use only a scythe and a 'b', worked into the letter W, to evoke St Walstan of Bawburgh.

The compilation of this book relied, as always, on the help, mild encouragement and unfettered criticism of my husband, Christopher, who has accompanied me hither and yon in search of the elusive St Walstan. This, he hopes, will be my last word on the subject!

CT
Rendham, 2004

ACKNOWLEDGEMENTS

Dr John Blatchly (for his generous sharing of unpublished research)

Bodleian Library

Roy Brigden (Keeper of the Museum of English Rural Life, University of Reading)

Revd David Dewick (at Bledlow)

Professor Eamon Duffy

Ken Farnhill

Dr Miriam Gill

Janet Gordon (for information about the Wooster family)

Hamish Grant (of Rongai, Kenya)

Robert Halliday

Professor Christopher Harper-Bill (for smoothing a path to the Bodleian)

Dr John C Henderson (Royal School of Church Music)

Dom Philip Jebb (Downside Library)

the late Dennis King

Michael King (Kings of Norwich)

Lambeth Palace Library

Anne Marshall (Associate Lecturer, The Open University, who raised the possibility of St Walstan at Gisleham)

Susanne McClelland (information relating to Stanford Rivers)

Betty Martins (Editor, Bawburgh News)

Professor Nigel Morgan

Norfolk County Council Library Services

Peter Northeast (for his advice and help in connection with will transcripts)

Margaret Osborne (Bishop's Library, Northampton)

Clive Paine (for information relating to St Mary's Bury St Edmunds, and the Gislingham will)

Monica and Cliff Robinson (for information about Bledlow, Buckinghamshire)

Professor David Rollason (for his original English translation of *De Sancto Walstanus Confessore* and permission to republish)

Revd Ray Simpson

Sally Simpson and St Michael's Workshop (Bowthorpe)

Suffolk County Council Library Services

Roy Tricker (for the discovery of St Lawrence in Norwich and his unfailing enthusiasm and support)

Victoria & Albert Museum

Peter Ward (for permission to reproduce the Holy Picture)

Kate Weaver (Churches Conservation Trust)

Chapter 1

The Legend

DURING THE THOUSAND YEARS that the legend of St Walstan and his mother St Blida has endured, various and numerous versions have emerged. There is no primary source for the Life of St Walstan and the basis for all of these many interpretations – or Lives – over nine centuries is the Latin Life, first published as one of the fifteen 'new' lives in Wynkyne de Worde's 1516 *Nova Legenda Anglie* (NLA). The NLA in turn owed a debt to John of Tynemouth's *Sanctilogium* begun in 1340, which was used in the 1450s by Friar Capgrave for his *Legends*. Carl Horstman republished the Latin Life, *De S Walstano Confessore*, in the 1901 edition of the NLA and a thorough investigation of the sources can be found in his Introduction. (See *In Search of St Walstan* for a fuller discussion of the origins of the Latin Life and Capgrave's *Legends*.)

De S Walstano Confessore was extracted from the 1901 NLA and published (in Latin) by M R James in 1917 (see bibliography). In 1995 an English translation, by Professor David Rollason, was published for the first time. While there are a few differences between the Latin Life and the much later English Life of 1658 (see Chapter 2) it is basically the same sequence of events and there can be little doubt that the English Life owes its story to the NLA. The chief

*(Opposite page) 1940s postcard of a Victorian print depicting St Walstan receiving the death message near to **Taverham Church**.*

difference between the Latin and English version is the additional eleven miracles (English) and the change of Walstan's birthplace from Bawburgh (Latin) to Blythburgh (English).

The name and nature of the original author of the pre-1516 Life of St Walstan is lost in time, but is likely to have been a monk from the Benedictine Priory in Norwich, which had jurisdiction over the Shrine Chapel at Bawburgh, in one form or another, from the early 1200s until the Dissolution of the Monasteries (see Blomefield for summary and references). If, as we are told in the Latin Life, St Walstan died in 1016, then it is probable that an account of his life would have been written at that time and circulated to surrounding parishes, notably Barnham Broom and Bowthorpe. This original, written prior to 1235, when the patronage of Bawburgh was given to the monks in Norwich, was conceivably that which formed the basis for the NLA contribution and for the English triptych that was created to grace the Shrine Chapel at Bawburgh. (A fuller and detailed discussion of the origins of the NLA Life, and of the part played by Friar John Capgrave, can be found in the 1901 NLA Introduction and in *In Search of St Walstan*, Chapter Four: The Search for Witness.)

The following is the 1995 translation of *De Sancto Walstanus Confessore* (Concerning St Walstan the Confessor) from the 1901 NLA. It is translated by Professor David Rollason and published with his kind permission. Carl Horstman, editor of the 1901 NLA, corrected the 1516 text where he thought there were errors but his corrections did not significantly alter the meaning. The endnotes included here highlight the chief differences between this and the 1658 English Life and did not form part of the original 1995 publication. Except where stated, all endnotes pertain to the English Life, using the most accessible version, i.e. M R James, 1917 (which uses the 1658 Walston spelling as opposed to the more usual Walstan) with references to copies made by Canon J C Morris and Fr Frederick Husenbeth. It will be observed that the language of the English Life (stated to be a copy of the original triptych) is obscure and poetic.

ST WALSTAN THE CONFESSOR
De Sancto Walstanus Confessore

St Walstan, a man acceptable to God, was born in the southern part of Great Britain in the vill of Bawburgh.[i] He derived his parentage of distinguished royal stock, his father being called Benedict, his mother Blida.[ii] From his earliest childhood, he showed himself in the true intention of his mind to be obedient to the divine will in all things. He showed himself full of the grace of humility towards the greatest and the least, devoid of all pride and arrogance, striving with all his mind and in all honesty to be humble and virtuous with dove-like simplicity.

When he reached the age of twelve, imbued in the spirit by divine inspiration and by the evangelical teaching, 'He who will not renounce all that he has, cannot be my disciple', and having received general permission from his parents, St Walstan renounced against their will all right of royal succession which he was entitled to thereafter.[iii] And so that he might be at leisure to devote himself more freely to prayer and other acts of contemplation without the pomp of the world, he left his birthplace, and did not delay to reach northern parts as quickly as he could.

In the name of Christ St Walstan bound himself in servitude and as it were in the strictness of obedience to a certain inhabitant of the vill of Taverham so that he should humbly serve him in all things.[iv] To such an extent was he inspired with the grace of divine virtue, that not only did he give to the poor the victuals supplied for his own sustenance, but he also distributed his clothes and shoes to needy and sick people, exposing himself barefoot to various sufferings.

---

[i] 'In Blyborow town ye child born was' places Walstan's birthplace in Blythburgh, Suffolk, rather than at Bawburgh in Norfolk

[ii] 'his father Benet, his mother Blythe by name'

[iii] 'A kings sonne … monished to forsake his kingdome free, he gave ready ear to ye godly message, from father, mother & kingdome he tooke passage'

[iv] '… northward his journey he take, a husband he meeteth, and of convenient treate fully agreed, they goe to reape wheate'

When one day a certain pauper asked alms of St Walstan and he was moved with great piety, he gave his own footwear to the pauper, on condition that the pauper should not reveal the gift to anyone. But as it has often been said, no pestilence is worse than the familiar enemy, it happened that the evil and most pernicious wife of the man whom St Walstan was serving found out about this gift. Astutely inventing some plausible necessity, she sent without delay the most holy confessor Walstan barefoot to the wood in order to load thorns and thistles onto a cart. But since Almighty God defends his faithful in all dangers, he miraculously visited St Walstan, so that he sat and boldly stood with the bare soles of his feet on the sharpest points of the thorns and thistles without suffering any harm from their punctures, as if they were roses redolent with the sweetest fragrance. In proper order, with the Lord's help, he gathered them together into the cart as that opprobrious woman had ordered. When the woman saw this miracle, she recognised the guilt of her iniquity and, throwing herself in floods of tears at St Walstan's feet, she begged forgiveness. The man of God benignly raised her to her feet and forgave her all the injury she had done to him.[v]

When his master saw the signs and miracles which St Walstan performed with God's permission, he came to love him devoutly, and publicly declared that he would make him his heir, since he had neither natural nor legitimate offspring. St Walstan rejected this promise with all his heart, and he asked for his labour nothing more than the offspring to be born to a certain cow, which he asserted would be sufficient reward. His master agreed at once to this request. When the time came, the aforesaid cow gave birth to two male calves, which St Walstan tended and fed as well as he was able, not out of human greed, but so that God's will might be fulfilled through them, as he had been divinely informed through an angel of God, that is that through them he should be miraculously led to the place where his body would be buried.[vi]

---

[v] The miracle of the thorns reads slightly differently but is virtually the same except that in the English Life the woman is *'punished & pricked wth thornes all about'*

[vi] 'This cow soon after calved shee twaine bullock calved … when these oxen were grown of age, his Mr delivered to Walston's possession'

When one Friday, St Walstan was scything with a companion in a certain meadow, the angel of God appeared to him and said, 'Brother Walstan, on the third day from today you will enter paradise', and at once vanished from his sight.[vii] Walstan thanked God for this divine revelation of his destiny, and without delay he respectfully asked and most devoutly received confession and with great contrition of heart the sacrament of the precious body and blood of Our Lord Jesus Christ and extreme unction from his priest.[viii]

On the next day, the Saturday, at the ninth hour, St Walstan threw his scythe from him and asserted that he was in no way permitted to work from that hour until the morning of the following Monday, because he could hear at that moment emanating from the celestial realms the sound of heavenly bells and the ineffable notes of trumpets. He said to his companion, 'If you are willing to believe, and to approach me and to place your foot devoutly on my foot, you will see with me the gate of heaven open and angels of God ringing the bells to the glory and praise of the holy and undivided Trinity.'[ix]

When the time of St Walstan's death came, that is the Monday of the following week, he went out as usual to work in the meadow with his companion.[x] There he called together his master and certain other honest persons, he fulfilled his last wish and commended his soul to God, the blessed Virgin Mary, and all the

---

[vii] '... ye angle of God to him there appeared soon, & shewd him yt he should depart ye life, peaceably passe without sword or knife'

[viii] English Life adds that the priest had no water with which to administer the sacrament 'there lacked liquour' and so they prayed to God whereupon a 'well in yt place sprang verament'

[ix] 'his fellow lifted his eye, & opened ear wide: he saw nor heard of ye heavenly thing till yt betooke him forth aside: his foot on Walston's set'

[x] English Life adds that on the Friday, the day of Walstan's death revelation, his employer heard a proclamation in Norwich to the effect that a king's son by the name of Walstan was sought by the authorities. The employer asks Walstan if he is the son of Blythe and Benet and is afraid for him, but Walstan reassures him saying that on Monday *'death shall depart us twaine in fayth'*

saints. He added in addition that his body should be decently placed in a cart, and that his two bulls should be yoked to it and, without any driver, should take it wherever God should ordain. At once he prostrated himself, and prayed to God, saying, 'O hope and salvation of the believers, O glory and rest of those who labour, good Jesus grant your servant this mercy, that if a labourer should have any infirmity or other bodily disablement, or if compelled by necessity anyone should reverently visit me with good will and in your holy name on behalf of brute animals, may be not be denied your help and, I pray Lord, may the brute animals be restored to health.'[xi]

When he had finished speaking, a voice from heaven said, 'O holy Walstan, what you have asked has been granted. Come from your labours to rest, come from your misery to salvation.' Those who were present with St Walstan when he went up to heaven and left this world are most veracious witnesses to the fact that it was as if a dove whiter than snow came out of the mouth of the saint and flew up to heaven, disappearing on high on a shining cloud.[xii]

Honest persons who were there put the holy body of Walstan on his cart as he had ordained, and the bulls took the road directly towards the wood of Costessey. On that journey the following miracle occurred. When the bulls with the holy body entered a pool of very deep water in the aforesaid wood, God granted this miracle for love and honour of St Walstan, that the wheels of the cart passed over the yielding and naturally liquid surface of the water as if over land or some other firm and consolidated material without sinking at all. The marks of those wheels are said even today to appear on the surface of the aforesaid water.[xiii]

[xi] English Life adds the succour of men, both priest and labourers, and also for Knights or men and woman labourers who might be sick or 'ache of bones'

[xii] English Life omits the dove, saying only 'The soul of Walston Angells bare to heaven'

[xiii] English Life adds that the cart and its cortege passed over the water without drowning

Another miracle also happened. When in the aforesaid wood, the bulls stood for a while with the body of St Walstan on top of a steep hill, a spring of water as a sign of grace for love of St Walstan appeared against the nature of the place (for until that time no water had been found there) and through divine mercy is still there today.[xiv]

The bulls went down from that place with the precious body towards the vill of Bawburgh. When they had come almost to the place where the body now lies buried, they made another stop in a certain place, where for love of St Walstan the divine piety made another spring of wonderful power against fevers and many other infirmities, which is still there today.[xv]

The body of the holy man Walstan was placed in the church of Bawburgh, which is dedicated in his name, and for love of him God performs diverse miracles.[xvi] For there the paralysed are cured, the blind receive sight, the deaf can hear, the mute speak, the lame walk, those with fever are relieved, the possessed are freed from demons, those deprived of their eyes and their genitals are found worthy to receive new members through the merits of St Walstan.[xvii] Not only are catholic people freed from various ailments by this saint, but also brute animals suffering from whatever complaints are restored to pristine health.[xviii]

[xiv] English Life says '*the one ox staled, a marvellous case: there sprang a well by Gods grace*'. The word 'staled' has been interpreted as both 'stalled' (came to a halt) or 'staled' (urinated).

[xv] English Life adds '*ye other ox staled; a well sprang anon next beyond ye Parsonage*', this being the 3rd well in the English Life and 2nd in the Latin Life, but advances the case for 'staled' to mean that the ox urinated.

[xvi] English Life adds that on arrival at '*ye toun of Bawburgh*' the '*Angells opened ye walls in hast*' so that the oxen, the body of St Walstan and all followers could pass through the 'closed' walls into the church interior.

[xvii] English Life omits 'their eyes or their genitals', saying '*Blind men made to see and looke on ye sunne, Crooked both & lame right up for to goe, ye deafe man perfectly his hearing hath wonne, damned spirit cast out of man also, Leprosy, Fevir, Palsy, wt many sicknesses mo be cur'd & heal'd in their holy place*'

xviii English Life lists 11 specific miracles, none of which appear in the Latin Life, and were clearly added to what became the 'popular' Life of St Walstan displayed in the Shrine Chapel for the edification of 14th- and 15th-century pilgrims.

Dearly beloved, let us commend therefore this solemn day of St Walstan, who that he might gain everlasting life, left transitory things; that he might live chastely, frequently afflicted his flesh with fasting and gave his victuals to the poor; and that he might remain in constant virtue and humility rejected the royal succession of his parents and bound himself to the service of simple rural persons. Oh St Walstan, justly are you to be praised in the church of God. Through the abdication of temporal things you can be compared to the apostles; through the penitential mortification of your flesh you are similar to the martyrs; through the giving of alms and the effusion of holy prayers you are a companion of the confessors.

That excellent man St Walstan migrated to the Lord in the year of the Incarnation of Our Lord 1016, on 30 May. Sighing after him, dearest brothers, let us follow in his footsteps along the paths of truth and justice and of perfect humility, that we may be worthy to come with him to the realm of light and glory, in which God reigns, world without end, Amen.[xix]

[xix] English Life adds that the Bishop of Norwich, together with priors and monks, went to bury Walstan and *'allowd him a Saint for ever more'* thereby confirming it to be a later, and uninformed, addition to the earlier Life. The first Bishop of Norwich was Herbert Losinga (1091) and a Bishop attending Walstan's funeral would have been Alfwine (or Alwin), Bishop of Elmham in 1016.

Chapter 2

Archdeacon Tenison and the English Life

IN THE AUTUMN OF 1658 an unknown scribe made a copy of an ancient parchment manuscript contained in a triptych, i.e. three hinged panels with sides able to fold over the centre or stand on its own. He entitled this copy *A History of St Walston* and wrote on it that the original was in the hands of a 'recusant' named Mr Clarke, of 'Beauthorp' (now Bowthorpe) in Norfolk, but that it belonged to the Church of Bawburgh. It has 75 seven-line stanzas and an envoy (the author's concluding words) of eight lines, 533 lines in all. This copy survived among a collection of papers given by Archbishop Thomas Tenison (1636-1715) to Edmund Gibson (1669-1748), when the latter was Lambeth librarian, catalogued as Lambeth Manuscript 935 (Item 8), and is extant in Lambeth Palace Library.

The triptych, though lost, is the second of only two known lives of St Walstan and, since the copy is in English, was presumed to be a translation of the earlier Latin Life (but with the obvious addition of the 11 miracles). Item 8 of the Lambeth manuscript – hereafter referred to as the English Life – is the only known copy of the lost triptych that would once have been kept in the Chapel of St Walstan at Bawburgh for the edification of pre-Reformation pilgrims and parishioners.

It is impossible to say when the triptych would have been inscribed, but the story of the English Life begins on 29 September 1658 when at least three key players were involved. These three were all in possession of the triptych at some point and, together with others in Bawburgh and Bowthorpe, had knowledge of its whereabouts since, probably, the destruction of the Shrine of St Walstan in 1538.

First there is the Scribe, who signed the document on the final page ('By Mr …), though heavy inking out later obscured his name. In what is probably a deviation from the content of the triptych he adds an eight-line envoy:

Goe, little treatyse, require folke of grace
yt shall have of thee inspection,
bee not too bold to appear in any place
of malapertnesse, other presumption
Thine Author simple thorow of affection
he meaneth well, pray ym yt shall thee read
with Ghostly support to doe correction
Thee to reforme as they see need. Finis

Quite what 'Thine Author' (did he mean himself or the author of the triptych?) had in mind when he wrote this has never been established, but he would appear benign rather than critical. His use of 'malapertnesse' could indicate that the Life of St Walstan might be subject to ridicule, rather in the manner of Bishop John Bale (1495-1563), who, at the time of the Reformation, delighted in verses pouring scorn on the religious beliefs of Catholics in the matter of saints and miracles. Among Bale's prolific writings in *English Votaries*, he indulges his tendency to the erotic by comparing Walstan to Priapus, a Greek God represented in a caricature of the human form, grotesquely misshapen, with an enormous phallus. The Scribe, by contrast, writes of 'affection' and 'meaneth well', although the reference to 'Ghostly support' has yet to be interpreted. Is he a 'ghost writer', admitting that he has changed words ('Thee to reforme') or is this subtle reference to the Holy Ghost?

Then there is Mr Clarke, said on the front page to be 'the owner' of the triptych. While there was a positive move to protect the identity of the Scribe, the same courtesy was not extended to Mr Clarke, who is blatantly and without compromise named as 'a Papist' and 'a Recusant' (an adherent of the old, displaced Roman Catholicism and a member of a persecuted minority). Not only was his identity given but also his place of residence, i.e. Bowthorpe.

Finally, there is Archdeacon Philip Tenison (1612-1661), who may well have commissioned the Scribe and was the most likely person to have taken possession of the English Life some time between September 1658 and his death in January 1661. There is no evidence of this, other than the fact that it eventually turned up in the papers of his nephew, Archbishop Thomas Tenison. Philip Tenison himself died at the early age of 48 and left no will. He did, however, have sight of the English Life as it is signed 'Norff', which could only have occurred between August 1660 and January 1661 (when Archdeacon). Was he merely clearing his desk following the events of the Restoration and, perhaps, closing his Bawburgh school?

No doubt there were others concerned in what might have been a clandestine operation to copy the triptych (it being a Catholic document in that it adorned the Shrine of St Walstan in pre-Reformation Bawburgh), but of the Scribe, Mr Clarke and Archdeacon Philip Tenison we can be sure. To date no further information has emerged about the fate of the triptych, how it came into the possession of Mr Clarke at Bowthorpe, or why it was not saved by the same route as the copy, i.e. in the papers of Archbishop Thomas Tenison. What it is reasonable to assume is that it was saved from the reformers in 1538 by a parishioner, who hid it from those who had come to burn the figure of St Walstan and other 'idolatrous' items. This happened in other places, as shown by Eamon Duffy in *The Voices of Morebath*, where items rescued from the parish church in 1538 resurfaced in the reign of the Catholic Queen Mary. Though unable to save the statue of St Sidwell, the Vicar 'took back to the vicarage a cloth painted with her image, the basin in which her light had burned'. How the Bawburgh triptych ended up in Bowthorpe will probably never be known,

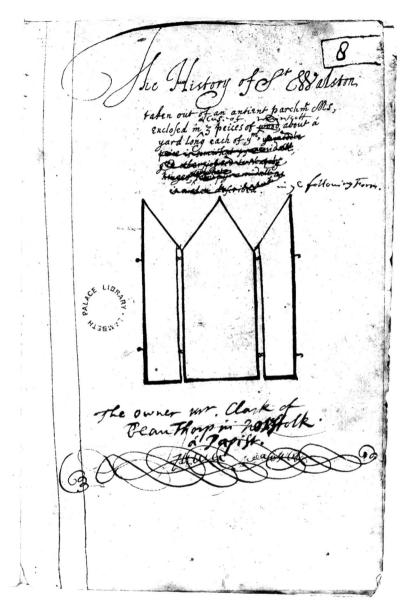

*The first page of **Item 8**, with corrections made by Archbishop Tenison and an outline drawing of the original triptych. (Lambeth Palace Library)*

other than the ecclesiastical connections between the two parishes would have provided a route for it to escape from the reformers as they ransacked Bawburgh Church.

Of the Scribe we know little, other than his being predictably male, but if we knew his name there is a chance of finding him in the parish records of either Bawburgh or Bowthorpe. Was he a cleric and, like Mr Clarke, a recusant who found sanctuary at Costessey Hall courtesy of the Catholic Jerninghams? Or was he a student of Philip Tenison's school in Bawburgh (of which more later)? It is entirely possible that modern technology could reveal the name of the Scribe if the will and finance existed among those authorities concerned who could be persuaded of the merits of the exercise. What the knowledge of the Scribe's name could add to the history of the English Life can only be speculative, but would be a welcome new piece in the jigsaw.

It is to be wondered if the Scribe copied the triptych faithfully or even if he transcribed it from Latin (which would account for the rather peculiar and obscure verse, described by Husenbeth as sometimes 'quite unintelligible'), although both Husenbeth and M R James both thought the latter unlikely, especially in view of it being pronounced a copy. In addition, the content of the miracles and the persons mentioned in them, e.g. Sir Gregory Lovell, would not have formed part of the Latin Life. Indeed, since Sir Gregory Lovell flourished around 1470-1500, it can be presumed that the miracle that concerns him, at least, dates from the latter half of the 15th century and therefore contributes to assessment of the triptych date. In 1917, M R James wrote:

With all submission to experts, I suggest that the date of the metrical life is quite late in the 15th century, and that it is modelled on the verse-legends of saints written by Lydgate, e.g. Edmund, Fremund, Margaret, Alban, etc.

The description of the triptych suggests it was like others of its type that were displayed in English places of worship, especially chapels and shrines to a particular saint, during the 1400 and 1500s when the pilgrim trade was at its height. It is unknown, however, if the triptych spelling of Walston used an 'o' between 't' and 'n' or whether the scribe changed it, although the two are

15 which is ye will of God to create all thing.
but stoode & abideth in himselfe musing,
who doth these miracles but God above
yt is to be worshipped of every creature,
then unkind man, looke yt thou him love
for it is his duty & thou ensure,
wth heart both & mynd demure;
who so saith Nay I say Yea
Quia ipse est Deus qui facit mirabilia.
O marvelous God sitting in thy throne
in high heaven passing all man's reason
whose man be sicke or groane,
by thee is relieved in duly season
neither yeilding love nor thanke it is great treason,
for thou hast provided in ordinations hea
yt to Thee all only honour sit & Gloria
                    AMEN.

Goe litle treatyse, require folke of grace
yt shall heare of theyr inspection,
bee not too bolde to appeare in any place
of malapert nosse other presumption,
thine Author simply thorow of affection
he meaneth well, pray ym yt shall yow reade
wth Ghostly support to doe correction
these To reforme as they see need.
                    Finis

Copied out of ye Originall
Sept. 29th Año dni 1658.

The originall is in ye hands of a Recusant Mr Clarke
&, as he saith, belongeth to ye Church of Bawburgh
                    North.

The final page of **Item 8**, *copied out of the original on 29th September 1658.* (Lambeth Palace Library)

acceptably interchangeable. In 1917, M R James thought the Scribe 'transcriber' rather than translator:

> *I cannot suppose that the transcriber has been at all faithful to the spelling of the original, but the copy is not a bad one … and only in a very few places do real blunders occur.*

The Scribe might simply have embellished the copy with his own style and interpretation and – it has always been assumed – was familiar with both the Latin Life and the additional miracles. This is not necessarily the case. It could simply have been an exercise set by a tutor to a student to improve his handwriting. After all, it has been agreed by those who have examined the copy that the Scribe undoubtedly executed it in a slap-dash fashion, with no particular thought for its place in posterity.

In addition, it has been assumed that execution of the English Life was done with a degree of secrecy and therefore haste: the triptych itself was old and probably difficult to decipher and belonged to the Catholic age which was disapproved of not only by state Protestantism but especially by the prevailing puritan regime. On 3 September – only 26 days previously – Oliver Cromwell had died and was succeeded as Lord Protector by his son. No one knew what might happen next or how Cromwell's son might perform. Perhaps this was the spur for whoever commissioned the copy, fearing that its discovery meant its destruction. Was there a fear among the people that there might yet be more upheaval in the legally enforced religious allegiances that had seen Catholicism supplanted by Henry VIII's English Church, followed by a rally of the Old Faith and persecution of Protestants under Queen Mary, and the backlash of non-conformity and Puritanism under Cromwell? The fact that his name is obliterated suggests that it was done for his own protection, though someone was careful to shift the responsibility of the triptych's ownership firmly into the Bowthorpe camp.

What if there was more than one copy of the triptych and Item 8 is the only survivor? Were there several students, all copying from the triptych – stood up on a table so that they could all see it – as part of a practise exercise in Philip

DESCENDANTS OF JOHN TENISON

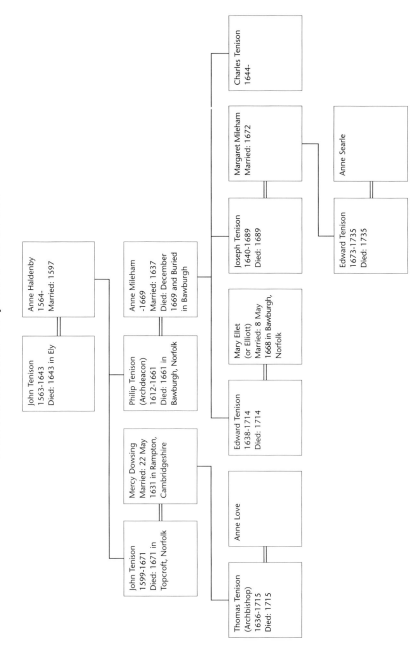

John Tenison
1563-1643
Died: 1643 in Ely

Anne Haldenby
1564-
Married: 1597

John Tenison
1599-1671
Died: 1671 in
Topcroft, Norfolk

Mercy Dowsing
Married: 22 May
1631 in Rampton,
Cambridgeshire

Philip Tenison
(Archdeacon)
1612-1661
Died: 1661 in
Bawburgh, Norfolk

Anne Mileham
-1669
Married: 1637
Died: December
1669 and Buried
in Bawburgh

Thomas Tenison
(Archbishop)
1636-1715
Died: 1715

Anne Love

Edward Tenison
1638-1714
Died: 1714

Mary Ellet
(or Elliott)
Married: 8 May
1668 in Bawburgh,
Norfolk

Joseph Tenison
1640-1689
Died: 1689

Margaret Mileham
Married: 1672

Charles Tenison
1644-

Edward Tenison
1673-1735
Died: 1735

Anne Searle

Tenison's Bawburgh school? Might the date of its transcription be coincidental, and therefore irrelevant, the triptych being no more than an amusing curiosity? If this is the work of a student it would account for the irregular spelling and lack of professional finish.

Mr Clarke was a recusant, a Papist, and possibly the man whose responsibility it was to protect the triptych: perhaps his family had hidden it from the reformers in 1538 and successive generations had guarded it for 124 years. How? Where? Why? Who persuaded him to let it be copied, and why should it have happened in 1658? Why did the copy prevail while the triptych was lost? Was Mr Clarke ordered to surrender it and if so by whom and to what authority? Or had he tired of it and donated it to Archdeacon Tenison's students as a novelty to be copied and disposed of? He is credited as the 'owner' of the triptych on the first page and on the last page he says that although it is in his hands, it 'belongeth to ye Church of Bawburgh'. Is Mr Clarke, too, attempting to disclaim ownership either through fear of retribution or purely from disinterest?

These and other questions keep us guessing, wondering and perhaps quietly hoping that one day the triptych, or other copies, might be found. It would surely have been destroyed in 1538 had it not been removed from the Chapel of St Walstan when Henry VIII ordered the destruction of the shrines. Many people in the parishes of Bawburgh, Bowthorpe and Costessey must have been involved in this story, but without Archdeacon Philip Tenison it is doubtful that posterity would ever have known about the triptych and the copy would not have survived.

Philip Tenison was born at Downham (near Ely in Cambridgeshire) on 26 April 1612, into a family long steeped in academic and religious learning and a culture of church service (see family tree diagram left). His father, the Revd John Tenison (1563-1643), could trace his family safely back to at least the middle of the 15th century and his father and grandfather were educated men with social status. In 1597 John Tenison was presented by Elizabeth I to the Rectory of Downham, just three miles from Ely Cathedral (called Little Downham to distinguish it from Downham Market in Norfolk). In the same year he married

Anne Haldenby, the eldest daughter of Philip Haldenby, whose ancestors were from an old Yorkshire family of royal descent. Their eldest son, John (born 1599) had an eventful and high-profile career. In 1624 he was appointed curate to Cottenham (Cambridgeshire) which living was later sequestered by the Westminster Assembly. The sister and brother-in-law of Oliver Cromwell resided in Cottenham Rectory during the Interregnum and, it is thought, were joined there by the Protector himself on several occasions. John was appointed Rector of Mundesley (Norfolk) but during the Commonwealth was turned out of the living as an ardent adherent to King Charles the Martyr. At the Restoration John Tenison continued to act as curate for some years thereafter, eventually moving to Bracon Ash (near Norwich) where his son, Thomas, was presented in 1661. Thomas Tenison (1636-1715) became Archbishop of Canterbury in 1694 and crowned Queen Anne in 1702.

John and Anne's second son, Philip, was to become Archdeacon of Norfolk and destined to end his days at Bawburgh, where he founded and ran a school, having suffered under the Puritan rule and been ousted from Hethersett and Foulsham.

Philip Tenison was admitted to Trinity College, Cambridge in 1631 and after being awarded a BA (in 1632) and an MA (in 1635) he became Vicar of Barton (Ely) in 1637. In the same year he married Anne Mileham of Burlingham (Norfolk), variously described as the daughter of Sir Gregory (or Gregorius) and Dorothea Mileham, Edric and Dorothea Mileham, and Edward and Dorothy (née Hobart) Mileham. The Mileham family of Burlingham (Norfolk) are numerous and a goodly proportion of the female members – both by birth and marriage – are named Dorothy. However, whether or not Anne was the daughter or sister of Sir Gregory, or whether she and Dorothy Mileham were sisters or half-sisters, they were related in some way. Dorothy Mileham married Sir Thomas Browne (philosopher, physician and author of Religio Medici who was knighted by Charles II) at Norwich in 1641. The Browne and Tenison families were close and included Philip's nephew, Thomas Tenison, the future Archbishop. Edward Carpenter points out:

It was [the family] connection with Sir Thomas Browne which, probably, led to
Tenison's being chosen upper minister of St Peter Mancroft in Norwich in 1673,
this church being then, as since, the centre of religious life in the city …
a portrait of the future Archbishop still hangs in the sacristy of the church.

Thomas Tenison edited tracts written by Sir Thomas Browne and later contemplated writing his biography, but gave up the idea as his other work as a rising star in the Church of England pushed it to one side. However, it is worth noting that when Sir Thomas Browne died in 1682 his son, Edward Browne, passed his father's unpublished papers to Thomas Tenison (which, presumably, were to have assisted with the proposed, but never completed, biography).

Might this connection between the Browne and Tenison families be another route by which the English Life of St Walstan came to be in Lambeth Palace Library? Perhaps Philip Tenison had passed it to Sir Thomas at some point and it was among the papers given by Edward Browne to Thomas Tenison in 1682?

Philip Tenison, arch supporter of the King, had been appointed Rector of Hethersett (Norfolk) in 1647, from which he was ejected during the Rebellion to make way for one Jeremiah Coleman (who was buried there in 1658). He was imprisoned for a time in Norwich gaol but was eventually released and chose to live with his wife and family in Bawburgh. There, in spite of legislation that forbade clerics to set up 'shop' as tutors, Philip Tenison founded his school.

Who were his pupils: sons of East Anglia's county aristocracy, protestant clergy anxious to continue their studies, or local landowners who were either Royalists or recusants, or both? Was the Scribe one of these young men, sent to Bawburgh by his father anxious that he should continue to study during the Puritan years? The verse on the final page of the English Life suggests a youth with a playful and irreverent sense of humour. He writes 'not too bold to appear in any place of malapertnesse' (malapert is an ancient word for an impudent or saucy person, bold in speech or behaviour) and his work is often corrected. For example, his wordy description of the triptych is edited from seven lines to four by someone substituting '… in ye following terms'. Could this Scribe even have hailed from Blythburgh and mischievously inserted his own birthplace,

Blyborow town, instead of Bawburgh? The English Life is, after all, a copy and the only evidence that Blyborow appeared in the original triptych.

In May 1660 the lately restored King Charles II rode through London to the accompaniment of church bells and bonfires on street corners. The arms of the new Monarch were raised in churches across England and no doubt it was the pro-royal Philip Tenison who arranged that Bawburgh be among them. The Established Church soon re-established itself and Philip Tenison was presented to the Rectory of Foulsham (Norfolk), in compensation for 'his great sufferings in the late evil times', and on 24 August 1660 was appointed Archdeacon of Norfolk. But he was not to enjoy the Restoration, the end of Puritan rule, or his preferment for long: he died at Bawburgh in January 1661, aged 48. His brass in the chancel of Bawburgh Church is extant though it bears an incorrect death year, i.e. 1660. As he died in January 1661 it can be assumed that the engraver (who lived and worked in London, not Norfolk) simply made an error and the Tenison family were abnormally quick off the mark in commissioning the brass.

The Tenison family continued to live in Bawburgh for some years, Philip's son Edward marrying there in 1668, but although his widow Anne was buried at Bawburgh in 1669 it appears from the registers that she was living in Norwich at the time. In spite of there being several sons born to previous generations of the Tenison family, Philip's eldest son had no male heir, nor did Archbishop Thomas Tenison.

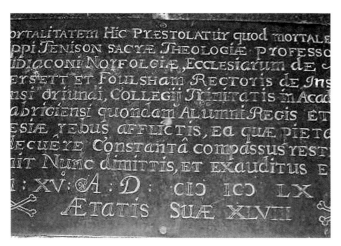

Inscription to Archdeacon Philip Tenison in Bawburgh Church, showing the incorrect year of death, i.e. 1660 (LX). (Betty Martins)

Philip's second son, Joseph, had a son by Margaret Mileham (from the same family as his mother Anne and his aunt Dorothy, who some historians claim as Margaret's half-sister). This son, the Revd Edward Tenison, became head of the family in succession to his cousin the Archbishop (who married but had no children) and was executor not only to his will but also to that of all the other male Tenisons. Both his mother and grandmother were Milehams, and he had free and easy access to papers on both sides of the family plus a sizeable quantity from Sir Thomas Browne's estate.

So how did the English Life of St Walstan find its way into Lambeth Palace Library? The Librarian there asserts that some of the over-writing is confirmed as belonging to the Archbishop, which means that he must have seen it. Did it come into his possession from Philip Tenison's paper, or from Sir Thomas Browne's?

In spite of his support for the King, the Archbishop (whose father-in-law Richard Love was Chaplain to King Charles I) was fervently anti-Catholic. Did he preserve the copy purely as an aid to his proposed biography of Sir Thomas Browne or did he have a personal interest in Bawburgh and the Life of St Walstan?

Alternatively, the copy might have been among the papers of Philip Tenison when the family moved back to Norwich and were kept together merely in the course of things; men of academia like the Tenisons cherish documents and writings and know their value in history. Philip's grandson, the Revd Edward Tenison, carried on the family tradition of entering the Church and was a man of letters. If he had come across the copy – or, come to that the triptych itself – would he have destroyed it as a remnant of Catholicism or might he have conserved it as a part of history? Until a few more solid facts emerge about the people and circumstances surrounding the English Life its story continues to flourish amid conjecture and supposition. Yet it remains one of the few tangible remnants of the cult of St Walstan and, as such, earns an exaggerated importance in the search for the historical and religious influence his and other such shrines had on the common people.

A panel on the rood screen at
Foxearth *is the only known*
pre-Reformation depiction
of St Walstan in Essex.

Chapter 3

Essex Gazetteer

TO DATE, THERE ARE THREE representations of St Walstan in Essex, one pre- and two post-Reformation, plus a medieval link between Bawburgh and the Augustinian Abbey at Little Dunmow.

When in 1995 the rood screen painting at Foxearth was included in the St Walstan gazetteer it was the first time that Essex had been included in such a list and, apart from Gresford, it was (and still is) the only extant pre-Reformation representation outside Norfolk or Suffolk.

Since 1995 the window at Stanford Rivers has come to light and as recently as 2002 the stained glass at Kirby-le-Soken was added to the Essex list.

St Blida is not found in Essex in any connection, ancient or modern.

FOXEARTH, SS Peter and Paul

A panel on this **rood screen** is the only known pre-Reformation depiction of St Walstan in Essex. Although the original screen is early 16th-century, the figures were much restored during the incumbency of the Revd John Foster, JP, who was Rector from 1845 until his death in 1892. The male figures on the south side (left to right) are Christ, SS Alban, Walstan, Felix, Edmund and Augustine the Doctor. St Walstan wears a red robe, a dark grey full-length cape, and holds a scythe. John Foster added embellishments in the form of a gold crown, sceptre and neck seal.

*Window at St Michael, **Kirby-le-Soken**.*

Foster, a high churchman in the Tractarian tradition, was a philanthropist who inherited a fortune from his mother. He owned most of the parish of Foxearth and spent large sums of his own money in 'restoring' the church, as well as improving the Rectory and building a village school.

Norman Scarfe attributes the panel as 'early Tudor' and describes the renovations as harsh, but the figure of St Walstan does not seem to have been fundamentally altered. There is no reason to suggest that the Revd Foster would have changed the original identity of the screen saints.

REFERENCES:

Shell Guide to Essex Norman Scarfe (Faber & Faber, 1968)

Something About Foxearth Church Kenneth Nice (1993)

The debt owed to Rev Foster East Anglian Daily Times (20 July 1998)

Royal Commission on Historical Monuments (England) *An Inventory of the Historical Monuments in Essex 1, North-West* (1916)

KIRBY-LE-SOKEN, St Michael

On the **north wall (chancel end)** are the remains of a doorway that was once possibly the Priest's door, which is flanked by two windows. One contains **stained glass** depicting the Annunciation and the Nativity and the other, dated 1962, contains four saints – Osyth, Walstan, Elizabeth of Hungary and Fiacre. The inscription reads:

> *To the Glory of God William Harry Cheeld d. 1952 and in memory of Katie his wife d. 1957.*

The initials 'AW' are entwined with a stag's antlers in the St Osyth panel and dated 1962. Stag antlers are a recognised symbol of the late 7th-century St Osyth of Chich, Patron Saint of Essex. St Osyth was reputedly an Anglo-Saxon princess who married Sighere (circa 664-675), king of the East Saxons, but during their wedding feast Sighere caught sight of a stag passing the house. Without a thought for his bride he called to his men and rushed off in pursuit. Osyth, not unreasonably, decided that hunting was more important to Sighere than his marriage and took herself off to the nearest nunnery. Eventually Sighere gave his wife the village of Chich, where she founded a nunnery and gave her name to the village.

St Walstan is depicted crowned, holding a scythe and described as 'Confessor & Husbandman'. He bears a Crusader's cross on his tunic and wears what appear to be knee-high chain-mail stockings and leather slippers.

The Cheeld family came to Essex from Kent in the mid-1800s and lived in the Clacton-on-Sea area, where they were involved in smallholding and the catering industry. The inclusion of SS Walstan and Fiacre in the window commemorates the family's links with the land and its cultivation. (St Fiacre is a 7th-century hermit and patron saint of horticulturists.)

St Walstan is among a host of saints in St Michael's, mostly in 20th-century glass, including SS Aidan and Cedd in the (1935) 'Iona' window. In a window to commemorate the life of a church organist, who died in 1967, are St Ambrose, St Gregory, Giovanni da Palestrina and Johann Sebastian Bach (the last two being composers). The west window in the south aisle is dedicated to St Francis.

REFERENCES:

Parish Church of St Michael, Kirby-le-Soken (c 1970s)

The Friends of St Michael's Church, Kirby-le-Soken, Essex (undated)

www.stmichaelskirbyessex.co.uk

LITTLE DUNMOW

The first known link between Little Dunmow and Bawburgh is to be found in the Cartulary of Dunmow Priory for April 1445. There is recorded the award of a flitch (or gammon) of bacon to Richard Wright, yeoman farmer from Bawburgh, near Norwich.

There was a tradition at the priory (which continues in a modified form today) whereby a married couple with proven fidelity was awarded a flitch of bacon (although in 1445 only Richard Wright is mentioned, his wife goes unnamed). The Prior would award the flitch to all those who were married a year and a day and never repented the marriage, either sleeping or waking. In his book on the history of the Dunmow Flitch, Francis Steer points out that the award to Richard Wright was not only the first on record but was one of only five known cases where the prize was logged in the priory's records up to 1751. The Cartulary entry (in Latin) translates:

> *Memorandum, that one Richard Wright, of Bawburgh next Norwich, in the County of Norfolk, yeoman, came here and pleaded for the bacon of Dunmow on the 17th day of April in the 23rd year of the reign of King Henry VI, after the Conquest, and was sworn according to the form of the gift aforesaid, … &c.*

Kneeling on two hard pointed stones in the churchyard, the recipient husband and wife swore an oath that they would never wish themselves unmarried again, after which they were carried round the priory churchyard and through the town amid cheers and acclamations, the flitch carried before them.

It was to be 22 years before another award was recorded, to one Stephen Samuel of the nearby parish of Little Easton. Either the Prior found it difficult to find couples who did not repent their marriage in their first year or the clerk forgot to make the entries!

REFERENCES:

Cartulary of Dunmow Priory (MS British Museum Harl/662)

Blomefield's Norfolk (Bawburgh entry)

The History of the Dunmow Flitch Ceremony Francis W Steer (Essex Record Office Publications, 1951)

Searching for St Walstan in Essex Carol Twinch (Essex Countryside, 1996)

STANFORD RIVERS, St Margaret

In the **east window**, dedicated on 22 June 1952, St Walstan kneels on the right hand of Christ (as the Good Shepherd). He is shown wearing a vibrant blue cape over a brown doublet, with a scythe and one of his calves (which is red and

*East window, St Margaret's Church, **Stanford Rivers**.*

white). On the left of Christ is St Margaret of Scotland (1046-1093), granddaughter of Edmund Ironside (who died in 1016, the same year as St Walstan). Margaret was one of the last members of the Anglo-Saxon royal family. (Occasionally Margaret of Scotland is confused with St Margaret of Antioch, who is reputed to have lived as a shepherdess, but Pope Gelasius declared her cult apocryphal in 494 AD.)

In one of the two outer panels is Caedmon, who had charge of the horses at St Hilda's monastery at Whitby. This Caedmon, the 'Sweet Singer', was said by the Venerable Bede to have suddenly received the gift of song at an advanced age, and thereafter wrote many hymns and religious poems.

The window is in memory of a local farmer, Henry Millbank (1880-1950), and bears the inscription:

To the Glory of God and in loving memory of Henry William Millbank who died on the 19th May, 1950, aged 69 years. He was Churchwarden from 1906 till 1950.

The Very Revd G H Martin, Provost of All Saints' Cathedral, Khartoum, and Archdeacon in the Northern Sudan, dedicated the window, and the Reverend Canon E H Gallop, Rector of Bobbingworth and Rural Dean of Ongar, conducted the Service.

Henry Millbank was not only a farmer but also took an active role in public service. He was a founder member of the Ongar Young Farmers Club, a prominent and long-standing member of the National Farmers' Union and, in addition to his farming commitments and duties as a Justice of the Peace, was a Churchwarden at St Margaret's for 44 years.

REFERENCES:

The Ancient Parish Church of St Margaret, Stanford Rivers, Essex (undated)

Order of Service for the Dedication of the East Window of St Margaret's, Stanford Rivers, on Sunday 22nd June 1952

Searching for St Walstan in Essex Carol Twinch (Essex Countryside, 1996)

16th-century screen painting, **North Burlingham.**

Chapter 4

Norfolk Gazetteer

PRE-REFORMATION EVIDENCE for the cult and legend of SS Walstan and Blida is strongest and most frequent in Norfolk. St Blida is to be found only in Norfolk: her origins and following limited to Cawston, Martham and Norwich.

Fr Frederick Husenbeth made the original all-Norfolk list of pre-Reformation representations of St Walstan in 1850. It consisted of Burlingham St Andrew, the panels formerly in St James' Norwich, Ludham, Barnham Broom, Sparham and Denton. He added that he thought it not unlikely that there were others and the most significant Norfolk addition is the screen painting at Litcham.

In 1905 Gresford was added by Bryant in *Norfolk Churches*, the first site outside Norfolk to be listed.

In 1995 the first gazetteer was published (*In Search of St Walstan*), which included post-Reformation sites as well as Anglican and Catholic places of worship, secular imagery, and sites outside Norfolk. Such alterations, corrections and additions to the 1995 version as have become necessary are included here. Principal Norfolk additions are Binham, Gateley and St Laurence (Norwich) and the possibility of missing pre-Reformation screen paintings at Bawburgh and Martham. The research now being done by Dr John Blatchly on flint flushwork on East Anglian churches points to the possibility of St Walstan being discovered on at least two Norfolk churches – Fakenham and Garboldisham – and in worked stone at Erpingham.

Sisters from Ditchingham Convent lead the pilgrimage across the fields from Algarsthorpe, 1996.

Since 1995 additional evidence has surfaced that shows what the Shrine Chapel at Bawburgh might have contained, thanks to more wills being transcribed. Robert Clarke (1503) left 2 shillings towards the decoration of an image of St Walstan in Bawburgh Church and for silver shoes to be made for him; Thomas Shemyng the elder (1505) leaves 10 shillings 'to paint the saint's image' in the church; and Helen Russell (1472) leaves money for the chapel.

The lost chapel at Algarsthorpe turns out to have been more concerned with the story of St Walstan than merely a stopping-off place for pilgrims on their way from Wymondham and surrounding villages. In medieval England any connections with royalty or the aristocracy were exploited to the full and the inclusion of Sir Gregory Lovell in one of the English Life miracles is just such an example.

The Prayer Cell at Bowthorpe is unique in that its 20th-century icon was inspired spiritually, rather than in memorial. The fact that it is an on-going, living and breathing place of contemplation and respite in a burgeoning

Norwich suburb reflects the pre-Reformation type of worship that is evidenced by the English Life, even though here it is ecumenical, rather than Roman Catholic, by nature. There are several post-Reformation representations of St Walstan but that at Bowthorpe has an unparalleled degree of spirituality, as evidenced by the Emmaus Walk between the Bowthorpe Worship Centre and St Walstan's Well, Bawburgh (in May 2001).

[An Emmaus walk is a biblical meditation, which is done with another person, talking together on the outward journey and silent on the return journey. Its name derives from the story in Luke 24:13-35, where the disciples walk to Emmaus. The Emmaus movement was started 25 years ago in America.]

St Walstan

ALGARSTHORPE, Chapel of St Mary Magdalene

The tiny hamlet of Algarsthorpe, close to the boundary of Marlingford and lying west of Bawburgh on the south bank of the River Yare, was a stopping place for pilgrims approaching Bawburgh and had close **parochial links** with the Chapel of St Walstan. Its chapel had a chaplain to serve in it and priests to administer the sacraments. It is in the parish of Great Melton, where it has been since 1476. In Blomefield's time it was called 'Thorp'.

In Miracle 6 of the English Life, one Sir Gregory Lovell is cured of 'great sickness and great bone ache' by water from St Walstan's Well. Sir Gregory is found in Blomefield's *Norfolk* to have given a 'pitanciary' to the 'Monks of Norwich', being profits of two acres in Algarsthorpe ('Algerysthorpe by Bawburgh') which were given by Sir Gregory for a pittance in the monastery on his 'obit' day.

Sir Gregory's reward in his lifetime was not only to be cured of his ills but also to be featured in the devotional Life of St Walstan that once adorned his shrine at Bawburgh (at least, that is, he appeared in the copy, i.e. the English Life).

A pittance was a modest addition to the normally frugal monastic meal, often in celebration of a liturgical feast or other event in the life of the community. In this case it was to mark the obit day, or anniversary, which was to be the annual commemoration of Sir Gregory's death and would probably have included a re-enactment of the funeral service. As Sir Gregory did not die for another fourteen or fifteen years it might, perhaps, have been given at a time when he feared he might die.

The miraculous cure of Sir Gregory is recorded thus:

A knight Sir Gregory Lovell called,
With great sickness and great bone ache,
You shall hear what him befalled.
He was cast down in his bed, nake,
No man to heal durst him take,
Neither in city, burgh nor towne,
Full of pains from foot to the crown.

When he had spent both silver and gold,
Nothing ensued of amendment,
Moveable and unmoveable, he would have sold,
For ease and health had to his intent,
If God to him it would have sent,
Wife and children if he had not had,
And lived in poverty as God bad.

It happened by means of Walston and God's grace,
To muse in mind upon a night,
A meane make to holy Walston in that case,
For water to his well he sent as tyte,
Therewith him washed and also dyte
And remedy readily should have anon,
By the grace of God and holy Walston.

These things done as it is aforesaid,
Within ten days consumed the sickness
To visit St Walston he made abraid
Felt in his members life and quickness,
Not perfectly recovered, but found faintness
A little while continuing after in great wealth
And found in himself sure and perfect health.

Under Blomefield's Bawburgh entry, reference is made to an inventory made of the rectory in 1488 that included 'the meadows lying in Thorp'. It is likely these meadows were contiguous with Sir Gregory's two acres in 'Algerysthorp', the revenue from which he gave to the monks in 1491. He acquired the meadows in 1487 when Robert Toppe gave the Manor of Hakuns (or Hacons) to Sir Gregory Lovell (his nephew by virtue of the fact that his sister was married to Sir Ralph Lovell, Gregory's father) and to Anne Lovell, Sir Gregory's sister. In his own will Sir Gregory did not forget the Toppe family:

> To the said Margaret [his wife] to find a priest for my uncle Toppys and one for
> the term of 10 years after the death of the said Margaret.

The Algarsthorpe Chapel disappeared at the Reformation or before. In 1931 Messent wrote:

> Algarsthorpe now forms part of Great Melton and is situated to the north of the
> main road from Norwich to Hingham and Watton … [The hamlet] has now
> entirely disappeared, but when the foundations were being dug, some years ago,
> for farm premises to Chapel Farm a large number of skulls and other human
> bones were unearthed.

Messent gives the chapel as being dedicated to St Mary the Virgin, but on the Ordnance Survey map it is given as St Mary Magdalene's Chapel (situated due west of Chapel Farm) and Blomefield gives St Mary Magdalene.

Sir Gregory's patronage of Algarsthorpe (and St Walstan at Bawburgh) worked both ways: he used it to assuage his spiritual duties and the Shrine

Chapel was undoubtedly anxious to ally itself with a man who was both a local estate owner and a national figure. Between them, the family trees of Sir Gregory and his wife read like a *Who's Who* of medieval Norfolk and Suffolk. The Lovells themselves were of no mean importance, while Sir Gregory's wife, Margaret Brandon, was aunt to Charles Brandon, 1st Duke of Suffolk, and her mother was Elizabeth Wingfield (of Letheringham, Suffolk) who had family connections with the de la Poles, Earls and Dukes of Suffolk. (The arms of the de la Pole family can be seen in Bawburgh Church where medieval glass of the 15th century has been restored and reset in the nave window.)

Song sheet, Bishop's Pilgrimage.

Although there is no mention of St Walstan or Algarsthorpe in his will, Sir Gregory bequeathed his manor in Great Melton to his wife and thereafter his son, Thomas Lovell.

In September 1996 around 450 pilgrims led by the Bishop of Norwich, Sisters from All Hallows Convent at Ditchingham and the Revd Jonathan Lumby took part in a **'Children's Pilgrimage'** which began in Marlingford and set out from the church preceded by two white oxen (John Carrick's Horned Park cattle) and seven garlanded donkeys.

Jonathan Lumby wrote:

The crowd strung out, like a nation on the move, over the water-meadows south of the Yare. Later, it was a Galilean scene as all sat down to picnic on the hillside. Gingerbread donkeys, made by Mattishall baker Richard Norton, were given out – local equivalents of shells at Santiago.

Pilgrims picnicked just below Algarsthorpe and within sight of where the Chapel of St Mary Magdalene once stood. On arrival at St Walstan's Well the

Pilgrim Players, directed by Sue Page, enacted the last scene of Sheila Upjohn's libretto *St Walstan*, about the burial of the saint. Bishop Peter then addressed the large gathering of pilgrims and parishioners and led the circling of the dressed well.

To mark the occasion the parishioners of Marlingford presented the Bishop with a specially commissioned plate, designed by Graham Clarke of East Tuddenham.

REFERENCES:

Blomefield's *Norfolk*

Donkeys join in Pilgrimage Walk Jonathan Lumby (Norwich Diocesan News, 1996)

Will of Sir Gregory Lovell (4 May 1503) PCC:23 Adeane

Miscellanea Genealogica et Heraldica, Vol 2 (1st Series) pp 163-4

BARNHAM BROOM,
SS Peter and Paul

On this **15th-century screen panel** (left), St Walstan is shown in a green robe, with white (ermined) collar and cuffs, and two calf-like creatures at foot. He wears a golden crown and has a golden girdle. In his left hand he holds a scythe, at the base of which is a strickle (a wooden scythe sharpener, see Chapter 8).

Given Barnham Broom's proximity to Bawburgh it is not surprising to find St Walstan here.

(Above) Bawburgh Church and (right) village sign

(Betty Martins)

BAWBURGH, SS Mary and Walstan

Beside this ancient church, with its rare dedication, is the resting place of St Walstan. The site of **St Walstan's Shrine Chapel** can be seen on the (external) north wall.

Little survives from the long years of devotion, or from the great medieval pilgrimages, although the north wall of the church cannot have changed very much from the days when the reformers destroyed the chapel in 1538. In 1999 one of the final links, stretching back almost one thousand years, between the ancient chapel and the traditional site of St Walstan's Well was severed: the lane which led pilgrims from the hill to the site of the well was destroyed by development of the farm buildings on its border. The narrow way that dipped down below the roots of the bordering hedge, worn down by the feet of pilgrims who came to the well with hope and anticipation in their hearts, is now covered in tarmac and the age-old hedge ripped out. This small but ancient and evocative witness, together with the steps that led down from the churchyard, was not allowed to survive into the new millennium; modern pilgrims, the people of Norfolk, and the wider world are all the poorer for that. The well itself has a modern, dilapidated cover, and stands on privately owned land.

The path is mentioned in Blomefield:

… a tenement called 'Gybald's', abutting on the churchyard south, the rectory-house east, and on two ways leading to St Walstan's well, west and north.

Of St Walstan's Bush, a reputedly ancient thorn bush that stood close by the well, there is no sign.

Nor is there any trace of a **screen painting** of St Walstan that was said to have been in the church in 1958. The Revd C L S Linnell contributed a Selected List of Norfolk Churches to the *Collins Guide to English Parish Churches* and wrote of a 'screen with painting of the local St Wolstan [sic]'. There is no hint as to the age of the painting nor of its fate. No such painting exists now in the church and no local memory of it is known.

In 1819 the cult of St Walstan appears to have been in decline: the author of *Excursions in the County of Norfolk* writes:

[Bawburgh], at the east of this hundred, has been famous for the birth of St Walstan; but his history at this time would probably excite more contempt than interest or real information.

In 1905 Bryant credited other pre-Reformation survivals in the church:

There were formerly some good poppy-heads on the old benches, representing Angels, Saints and S Walstan.

We are not told when 'formerly' applied or what became of the bench ends. They might, however, have been removed during extensive church renovation in the 1890s during the incumbency of the Revd Gabriel Young (1845-1934). When Gabriel Young arrived at Bawburgh in 1892 he found the church in a 'deplorable state' and instigated extensive refurbishment. There is a package of information about Bawburgh and St Walstan that belonged to Gabriel Young but nothing is mentioned of either a pre-Reformation panel painting or bench end for St Walstan.

In the village a **wooden village sign**, carved by Alex Whammond, depicts St Walstan with animals and was erected in 1977 to celebrate the Queen's Silver Jubilee. The artist's monogram, 'AW' is entwined with 'Elizabeth II' on the reverse.

In 1981 a **carved figure** of St Walstan was dedicated in memory of Miss Margaret Young (daughter of the Revd Gabriel Young). It stands in the north-east section of the nave at the old entrance to the Shrine Chapel.

REFERENCES:

Collins Guide to English Parish Churches, edited by John Betjeman, (1958)

A Village Guide Carol Twinch (1981)

A Brief Guide to the History of St Mary & St Walstan (1982, 1987)

Walstan of Bawburgh, Norfolk's Patron Saint of Agriculture Carol Twinch (Media Associates, 1989)

St Mary and St Walstan Richard Butler-Stoney (1996)

Country Lane Gone for Ever (Eastern Daily Press, 24 June 1999)

www.bawburghnews.freeserve.co.uk

BEESTON-NEXT-MILEHAM, The Nativity of the Blessed Virgin

Although the painted figures on the **15th-century screen** are badly defaced, Eamon Duffy writes that one of those on the dado of the south side appear to have been carrying a scythe and is, therefore, identified as St Walstan.

REFERENCES:

Some East Anglian Clergy Charles Linnell (1961) [The Registers of the Revd John Forby, Rector of Beeston-next-Mileham, pg 24-44]

The Church of St Mary the Virgin, Beeston Richard Butler-Stoney (1992)

The Stripping of the Altars Eamon Duffy (1992)

BINHAM, The Priory Church of St Mary & The Holy Cross

On the **south wall**, sections of the **ancient rood screen panels** are displayed, where some of the original medieval paintings of saints are showing through the later painted black-letter texts of Cranmer's 1539 Bible. In 1989, Eamon Duffy identified one of these as St Walstan.

*Priory Church of St Mary & the Holy Cross, **Binham**, Norfolk*

This suggestion, though still open to investigation and confirmation, is important in establishing the extent of the cult of St Walstan: firstly, because of the prestige of Binham itself, in terms of East Anglia's religious centres; and secondly, in its proximity to Walsingham, a major destination at the height of religious pilgrimage in pre-Reformation Europe. Until now, the panels at Litcham and Beeston have been the closest surviving representations to Walsingham.

BOWTHORPE, St Walstan's Prayer Cell

A concrete **sculpture**, dedicated on 24 January 1989 by the Bishop of Lynn, stands at the entrance to the old forge, converted into a Prayer Cell, close to the Worship Centre and within sight of the ruins of St Michael's Church. One of the three panels of the concrete obelisk (designed by Jeremy Dearling, who had it cast and put in position by Lenwade Concrete) tells the story of St Walstan, while another depicts him in primitive design with scythe. 1989 was designated 'St Walstan's Year' by the Norwich Diocesan Board of Social Responsibility to coincide with British Food & Farming Year. The year-long celebrations began in Bowthorpe,

*Concrete sculpture outside the Prayer Cell at **Bowthorpe**.*
(Betty Martins)

where over three hundred years earlier the copy of the Bawburgh triptych (the English Life) had been copied under the eye of 'Mr Clarke of Beauthorp in Norfolk'.

At the Service of Dedication Jeremy Dearling said:

I was inspired by a carving I saw on St Michael's Mount, Cornwall … the design is executed in a primitive early Saxon style, the head being disproportionately larger than the body to denote importance. The figures on either side of the cross are sexless to enable observers to make up their own minds as to who stands beside their cross. The figures are expressionless, but contain their own expression.

Commissioned by the Revd Ray Simpson (Bowthorpe's first vicar and Free Church minister), the three-sided concrete memorial took several years to complete, each four-foot high side weighing half a ton. In *Bowthorpe – A Divine Accident* Ray Simpson recalls that it was while making pilgrimage at the wooden prayer cell of Switzerland's national saint, the farmer and layman Nicholas Von der Flue, that he heard an unmistakable command from God that he should reclaim the ruined blacksmith's forge at Bowthorpe into a Prayer Cell and dedicate it to St Walstan.

Ray Simpson was also the founder of the Bowthorpe Community Trust and is now Guardian of the Community of Aidan and Hilda, a network of Christians who seek to cradle modern spirituality inspired by the Celtic saints. He remembers that some time after its dedication, Rabbi Lionel Blue visited the Bowthorpe Cell:

[The Rabbi] was making a series of TV programmes on holy places of East Anglia. At the cell of Norwich's Mother Julian someone told him about St Walstan and the cell.

Together with a very weary crew, Rabbi Lionel Blue went to Bowthorpe. 'Jews aren't supposed to believe in saints,' he told Ray Simpson, but sat in contemplation in the Prayer Cell. Then he pronounced: 'Walstan is the answer to the yuppie. Every housing estate needs a saint.'

In 1989 those at St Michael's Workshop in Bowthorpe were asked to make wooden carved figures of St Walstan, using the Saxon design from the obelisk, and at that year's Royal Norfolk Show some 300 were given to Norfolk farmers on show day. The wooden carvings are still sold at the nearby shop, 'Hobby Horse'.

In 1992 the Norfolk Society, a branch of the Council for the Protection of Rural England, awarded a certificate recognising the value of the restored forge and its converted use as a community prayer cell.

In 2003 Sally Simpson wrote:

For the past 15 years the Prayer Hut has been available to all. It is used by children as well as adults. For short periods it has to be locked, if there's a bout of misuse, but on balance it is respected as a place of reverence and quiet.

Sally Simpson also recounts the story of two young tearaways who were sadly killed on stolen motorbikes in Bowthorpe. Afterwards the young friends of the two boys were bewildered and milled around Bowthorpe confused and not understanding what to do or how to assuage their grief. Sally invited them to take refuge in St Walstan's Prayer Cell, where many of them began to find a place where they could come to terms with what had happened, and why. The incident was recorded by Eldred Willey, who wrote of the two teenagers:

> *Riding without helmets, they lost control and hit a gate at about 70mph. Their bodies were discovered by a milkman early next morning. Just inside the door of the prayer cell, a crumpled piece of paper has been fixed with blu-tack: it is a tribute to the dead boys, signed by six of their friends.*

In January 2001, Norfolk County Council agreed to an official footpath which runs along an ancient bridle path and links Bowthorpe to Colney. It is intended that the path should be called St Walstan's Way.

REFERENCES:

The Ruined Churches of Norfolk Claude J W Messent (1931)

Bowthorpe, A Community's Beginnings (1982)

Giant Sculpture to Gentle Saint (Eastern Daily Press, 25 June 1987)

A Cell of Healing Eldred Willey (The Tablet, December 1991)

Person of the Millennium (Eastern Evening News, 30 December 1999)

This Norfolk Lad (Eastern Evening News, 6 January 2000)

Bowthorpe News (April 2000)

Do you remember …? (Eastern Evening News, 12 May 2003)

A Memorial with a Rich Rural History Sally Simpson (Eastern Evening News, 17 May 2003)

Bowthorpe – A Divine Accident Ray Simpson (2003)

Community of Aidan & Hilda (www.keeling.force9.co.uk)

COSTESSEY, Catholic Church of Our Lady and St Walstan

Land for the church and priest's house was made over to Fr Husenbeth in 1832 and the foundation stone was laid on 21 May 1834. Building began but was often held up due to lack of funds, so it was not until 26 May 1841 that it was finally opened and dedicated by Fr Husenbeth as the Church of Our Lady and St Walstan. Water from St Walstan's Well in Bawburgh was used in the dedication Mass. It was built under the patronage of the Jerninghams when their

TO THE MEMORY OF
THE VERY REVD.
F. C. HUSENBETH D.D.
PROVOST OF NORTHAMPTON
A WATCHFUL PASTOR
A LEARNED PRIEST
A ZEALOUS DEFENDER OF
THE FAITH. ON WHOSE SOUL
SWEET JESUS HAVE MERCY
DIED ON THE
31 DAY OF OCTOBER 1872
ALSO
MONSIGNOR GEORGE DAVIES

Gravestone of Fr Husenbeth,
Costessey.

own chapel at Costessey Hall became too small for the Catholic community, with additional public subscription. The total cost of building and furnishing the church was £4,415 7s 10¼d.

The church is built in the Gothic Revival/Early English style, the architect John Buckler from Oxford having designed the mansion in Costessey Park. Mr Buckler presented the baptismal font and James Grant made the coloured windows. The **east end window** is dedicated to *Walstanus* and depicts him in red robe and carrying a scythe. It is the earliest surviving example of St Walstan in glass (as no pre-Reformation example is extant).

In the churchyard is a memorial to Fr Frederick Charles Husenbeth, DD (1796-1872), author of *The Life of St Walstan, Confessor* and many other works of divinity including an edited version of *Butler's Lives of the Saints*. Born on St Walstan's Day (30 May) he was ordained a Catholic priest in 1820 and in that year went to Costessey Hall as Chaplain to Sir George Stafford Jerningham. He lived in Costessey for 52 years and was appointed Grand Vicar of Norfolk and Suffolk in 1827. Pope Pius IX conferred on him the honorary title of Doctor of Divinity. He died in the presbytery adjoining St Walstan's and is buried in the churchyard.

After Fr Husbenbeth died the Bishop was unable to find a priest to replace him and St Walstan's was closed for almost 40 years and the presbytery let to a tenant. In 1909 the Sanctuary of St Walstan's was restored and a year later Fr Francis Byrne came from Norwich to take charge of St Walstan's. In December of that year (1910) the Catholic Cathedral of St John's in Norwich was opened, and St Walstan's again dedicated to full parochial use. Fr Byrne became the first parish priest of St Walstan's.

Other Costessey sites include:

St Walstan's Well, Costessey Park is the site for the second of the **three wells** mentioned in the English Life, reputed to have been a stopping place for travellers and pilgrims until the 18th century. Although it has been dry for over 100 years, its flint lining can still be seen, with a diameter of 12 feet and a depth of six feet. The well is near to the point where the wagon carrying Walstan back to Bawburgh in 1016 crossed the River Wensum. Folklore has it that the wheel tracks could be seen on the river surface.

In 1992, the current editor of *Bawburgh News*, Betty Martins, visited the site with local historian Ernest Gage, but in spite of a long walk along the River Tud, negotiating barbed-wire fences, and a trek along a field edge, they were unable to locate the site. However, the following year, a second attempt was made in the company of Robert Atkins, when they found a large depression in the woods 'probably 12 feet in diameter … the walls were sloping and the flint lining was visible in parts. The base was quite firm.' The site places the well to the north of Owlhouse, Long Dale.

St Walstan's Close – a road leading off Bawburgh Lane. The latter once linked Costessey and Bawburgh but was sealed off in 1992 when the Norwich Southern Bypass was built.

St Walstan's Hall, Royal Norfolk Showground is the exhibitors' accommodation building, named to celebrate Walstan as Patron Saint of British Food & Farming Year, 1989.

Outside **Harvey's Funeral Home** in Norwich Road is a 1980s **double window** to SS Walstan and Edmund (pictured opposite). The design for St Walstan is based on that in the Catholic Church of Our Lady and St Walstan in Costessey.

REFERENCES:

The History of Costessey T B Norgate (1972)

An Account of St Walstan's, Costessey W T F Jolly (1973)

www.mdbtv.co.uk

www.cygnus.uwa.edu.au

DENTON, St Mary

Twelve panels from an **ancient rood screen**, likely to have formed part of the original **rood loft frontage**, were found in the porch room in a damaged state in 1845 and made into a chest the following year. The chest now stands in the chancel.

St Walstan is depicted (indistinctly but safely) on a panel, wearing a red robe with very wide sleeves and an ermined cape, scalloped round the border. He carries a scythe, the base of which is turned up ('with a shepherd's crook at its lower extremity', adds Husenbeth in his 'Life'). For a variety of reasons the 'crook' is unlikely to be a shepherd's crook, chiefly because there is no known example of a combined harvesting and shepherding tool, and because on closer examination that part of the scythe shaft that shows a hook also has a strickle handle protruding. It occurs a few inches up from the base and is unlike any other scythe depiction (see also Chapter 8).

The panels are defaced and each one measures only 12 inches by four inches. They probably came from the front of the rood screen loft, presumably at St Mary's. From left to right they show (east end) SS Agnes, Dorothy, (along the side) Jude, Peter, a Bishop, Unknown, Zitha with her rosary, Barbara, Edmund and Edward the Confessor. SS Walstan and Paul are on the west end. An extraordinary amount of gilt gesso pattern has survived and imbues the panels with lavish quality.

Keyser (1883) gives St James Major (more commonly St James the Great) as an alternative to St Walstan on the Denton screen but no other example can be found where a scythe is attributed to St James Major.

St Mary's is now a shared church between the Anglican and United Reform churches.

REFERENCES:

A Short Guide to the Church of St Mary, Denton Revd John Simpson (undated)

(Left) One of the twelve rood screen panels, made into a chest and kept in the church at **Denton***, depicts St Walstan.*

EASTON, Easton College

A **wooden sign**, carved by Harry Carter for the Norfolk School of Agriculture (now Easton College), was removed from the site for renovation some years ago. It depicts St Walstan in a red robe, lying on a cart being pulled by two oxen. It is hoped that eventually a fibreglass reproduction will be made for display inside the college.

ERPINGHAM, St Mary

Cautley gives a **crowned 'W'** on St Mary's tower in worked stone which, in the light of work done on flint flushwork at Fakenham and Garboldisham by Dr John Blatchly, is attributed to St Walstan.

Floriated 'W' at **Erpingham** *(John Blatchly)*

FAKENHAM, SS Peter and Paul

In 2004, John Blatchly suggested the **crowned letter 'W'** in the flint flushwork on the west entrance to the church as relating to St Walstan. It is, at the very least, representative of a saint whose name begins with W, since a crown over a letter would indicate a saint rather than a donor or other non-sainted person. It remains to be seen if any supporting evidence is forthcoming or whether other, similar such identification is confirmed.

[See Bibliography for John Blatchly's forthcoming work concerning flint flushwork on Suffolk and Norfolk churches.]

FRITTON, St Edmund (now in Norfolk but in Suffolk until 1974)

St Walstan is seen here in **modern glass** in the company of six other East Anglian saints – Olaf, Fursey, William, Felix, Ethelbert and Withburga. He has a scythe, a spade, and is bearded. The windows are 20th-century painted glass and were dedicated in 1905.

The Misses Jane and Lucy Cubitt gave the window containing St Walstan in memory of their father, the Revd Francis Cubitt. Other windows are in memory of their mother, Jane Mary Cubitt, who died in 1903, aged 97. Francis Cubitt was the first resident Rector of Fritton and served the parish for a stated 53 years. There is a slight discrepancy in the dates as, according to his gravestone, he died in 1882, which date appears in one of the windows in Roman numerals. However, in another of the windows the year of his death is given as 1889. There is more confusion at the '53 years' which should, therefore, be 51 years, the patronage having been bought from the Old Manor by the Cubitt family in 1831. Francis' son, Major Frank Cubitt gave the east windows when he was patron of the benefice.

The shortage of facts relating to the commissioning and installation of the windows is due in part to the removal of Fritton from Suffolk to Norfolk in 1974.

GARBOLDISHAM, St John the Baptist

In 2004, John Blatchly suggested the inclusion of St Walstan in two exterior **flushwork panels** at St John's, Garboldisham. A panel containing 'St' is followed by another with the letter 'W' and is found in knapped flint and freestone panels (called flushwork) at the base of the north wall of the tower. A second, smaller panel containing the letter 'W' is also found between St and MR (*Sancta Maria*).

Supporting evidence for a following to St Walstan at Garboldisham appears in Blomefield:

> *In 1506, John atte Cherche of Garboldesham was buried in the churchyard of*
> *All Hallows there, and gave 8 marks for an obit for a year, and 40s for a pilgrim*
> *to go to St James in Gales, in the next year of grace; and to a pilgrim to St*

*At **Fritton** St Walstan is found in company with six other East Anglian saints.*

Thomas of Canterbury 3s 4d and to a pilgrim to St Mildred 12d and to a pilgrim going to St Walstone's 6d.

That there was pilgrimage traffic passing through the village is clear; Blomefield points to one street that (in 1413) was called 'Palmer's-way, I suppose it is that which leads from Gatesthorp-gate, by which the pilgrims used to pass in pilgrimage to our Lady at Walsingham'. St James 'in Gales' refers to James the Great (of Compostela in Galicia) and the sums and distances are in proportion.

[A palmer was one who wore a representation of a palm branch as a token of pilgrimage to the Holy Land. In the Middle Ages, Palm Sunday was celebrated by the blessing of the palms in an elaborate rite and followed by a procession which left the nave by the north door and processed through the churchyard before returning through the south door.]

John atte Cherche was buried in All Hallows (All Saints) churchyard, just north of St John's, although that church is now a ruin. Before 1280, when the advowsons were joined, the upkeep of both churches was maintained by the respective Manors in which they stood, but in 1450 the Rector of St John's, Master John Halle, petitioned that the two churches be consolidated so they might be served by one Rector with a single income. Blomefield writes:

[All Saints] was officiated in till the death of Mr Vilet in 1726, from which time service was left off by degrees; and upon a petition of the patrons, incumbent, and parishioners, in 1734, license was obtained of the Bishop to suffer it to dilapidate, upon which the roof of the nave was unthatched (etc).

Further investigation revealed that the antiquary, Thomas Martin (1697-1771) had previously inspected the lettering at St John's and made a sketch that indicates the two left-hand strokes of the W are taken as a lower case 'b', while the right-hand stroke represents a

*'W' for St Walstan at St John the Baptist, **Garboldisham**.*

scythe – therefore, St Walstan of Bawburgh represented by a 'W'. Thomas Martin would have known about St Walstan through his friendship with Blomefield.

The element on the left of the 'W' panel could be an ear, or ears, of corn and thus another clue towards identifying Walstan.

Lettering on the north-east buttress of St John's tower is 'mh' (Master Halle) and 's (in reverse) w' (St Walstan) between the arms of a cross fleury, suggesting that John Halle's advower was St Walstan. (Elsewhere, on the north face, MIH appears for Magister Johannes Halle.) Continuing the agricultural theme, at about the same time the west tower of All Saints was built or rebuilt with panels for a shearman and a woolcomber.

Further conclusions on this flushwork will be found in John Blatchly's forthcoming book (see bibliography).

REFERENCES:

Church Notes Thomas Martin (c 1740) SROB 1183 folio 3

Church of St John the Baptist, Garboldisham Simon Cotton & Roy Tricker (undated)

The Church of St John the Baptist, Garboldisham: A Brief Guide (c 2000)

Blomefield's *Norfolk* (Vol 1, pg 270)

GATELEY, St Helen

A 1939 **reredos panel** of St Walstan is one of the most colourful of modern times. The vibrant red, green and gold, with vertical black and gold twists between the panels, makes for a startling effect which cheers up the inside of St Helen's and hints at what pre-Reformation decoration might have looked like when the art work was new. St Walstan is depicted here as a dreamy, fair-headed youth, with Anglo-Saxon overtones, and is reminiscent of the nearby Great Ryburgh transept screen painting of the 1920s. The spade is deployed as the specific emblem and the reredos also depicts SS Withburga, Etheldreda, Helen, Hugh and Felix, and has the symbol of the Holy Trinity above.

REFERENCES:

St Helen's Church, Gateley Richard Butler-Stoney (1995)

A panel of a 20th-century **Gateley** *reredos depicts a youthful St Walstan.*

GAYWOOD, St Faith

St Walstan is depicted here in an early **20th-century wood pulpit carving**. He has a Bible and – uniquely – a dog as his specific emblem and holds a staff rather than a scythe. The oak pulpit, carved by Mr N Hitch of London in 1909, depicts SS Dunstan, George, the Good Shepherd, Walstan and Nicholas. It is engraved 'In Dear Memory of Thomas Edward Bagge'.

There seems to be no particular reason for Walstan to have been included, but since the church has been enlarged from the original Norman building it is possible that the choice reflects an icon from the earlier period. There is a strong representation of East Anglian saints in the church, which incorporates the parishes of Mintlyn and Bawsey, united with Gaywood in 1937.

The dog is a substitute for the usual calf, or calves, and is better attributed to the 6th-century St Wendelin, a Patron Saint of Shepherds and peasants in Germany, who was also invoked on behalf of sick cattle. In *Emblems*, Maurice and Wilfred Drake give thirteen examples of the dog emblem, including the greyhound of St Ferdinand (whose Feast Date is the same as Walstan's, i.e. 30 May) and the small white dog of St Bernard.

REFERENCES:

The Parish Church of St Faith, Gaywood Elizabeth James 1984

GREAT MELTON, All Saints

St Walstan is seen here in a **stained glass window** dedicated in 1930 to Anthony and Matilda Curson, a local farming family. He wears a blue tunic, an ermined (gold) cape, with scythe (including strickle) and sceptre, with two white oxen at foot. The inscription reads:

> *In Memory of Anthony Curson, Warden of this Church 1920-1929 – also of Matilda his wife – faithful servants of Christ. The gift of their children.*

The prominent strickle shown at the base of the scythe is very precise and pronounced for a modern example and appears to show an understanding of its

*Stained glass window at **Great Melton**, dedicated in 1930.*

practical application. The white calves are a close copy of those at Barnham Broom (although white not brown in colour) and have goat-like horns.

Given the historical links between the parish of Great Melton and Algarsthorpe, and the connections with Sir Gregory Lovell and the de la Pole families, it is possible that an ancient, pre-Reformation icon of St Walstan existed in the contiguous (but ruined) church of St Mary, once the 'sister' church to All Saints.

GREAT RYBURGH, St Andrew

St Walstan has a **panel** (pictured left) in the **south transept screen** that serves to partition St Thomas' Chapel. It is a memorial to those who fought in the 1914-1918 World War and, although early 20th-century, adopts an Arthurian style. As if to indicate that St Walstan was no slouch, the artist employs (literally) the spade as the specific emblem and shows his industry by placing a pile of earth at his feet, dug from the tiled floor. He has a halo instead of a crown and wears Arthurian-style clothing, similar to that at Gateley.

The grey, gold and muted colouring of the panels lends a peaceful air to that part of the church while brightening its darkness. The black and white tiled flooring appears to be part of the overall artistic design and has no particular significance.

St Walstan appears in company with SS Remigius, Guthlac of Crowland, Etheldreda, Andrew, Thomas, Withburga and Felix. He stands between SS Withburga and Felix.

REFERENCES:

St Andrew's Church, Great Ryburgh Richard Butler-Stoney (1992)

*Basic design of the **Kenninghall** window containing SS Felix and Walstan* (Kings of Norwich)

KENNINGHALL, St Mary

A **20th-century stained glass window** on the south side of the nave depicts SS Walstan and Felix. The window, by Kings of Norwich, was erected in memory of a local farmer, Edward Wood of Fersfield Lodge (1906-1966). The colours are bold and vivid, St Walstan shown in medieval clothing.

LITCHAM All Saints

This church was once a stopping-place for pilgrims on their way to Our Lady of Walsingham, and St Walstan is depicted here on the south side of the **early 15th-century screen**. There are 22 panels, each containing a saint: some are too badly defaced to be identified but Walstan is among those considered 'safe'. He stands between a rare depiction of the 3rd-century St Gereon (with book and falcon) and St Hubert (the hunter, kneeling

before the white stag of his conversion).

Keyser describes the Litcham screen but omits Walstan from the list of male saints.

LUDHAM, St Catherine

On the south side of the elaborately painted **15th-century screen** St Walstan stands between Edward the Confessor and St Laurence. The screen is dated 1493 and bears the names of John Salman and his wife Sicilie, who donated the sum of £14 for its construction.

Walstan is depicted as a kingly figure with ermined cape and red tunic, holding a scythe and a very strange sceptre for which there is no explanation. The image is similar to those at Litcham and Denton. SS Gregory, Jerome, Edward and Walstan are in a different hand from that of the other eight panels.

The Ludham image was used as a model for Taverham village sign and a 20th-century painting now in the parish church at Bawburgh.

REFERENCES:

St Catherine's Church, Ludham J M Snelling (1972)

(Above left) Screen panel, **Litcham** (Betty Martins)
(Left) Painting of St Walstan on the screen at **Ludham**
by Harriet Gunn (Bishop's Library, Northampton)

MARTHAM, St Mary

While there is no extant evidence of St Walstan at Martham, a reference exists which indicates that there might have been a **screen painting** there until the 20th century. In *A Supplement to Blomefield's Norfolk* of 1929 Dom Cam Bede writes:

> *St Walstan also occurred on a separate panel painting, preserved in the chapel dedicated to his mother, St Blide, on the South side of Martham Church. I have a painting of this panel given to me by a Norwich antiquarian, Mr Walter Piper.*

Although Dom Bede's papers at Downside Library have been searched for any other records of this painting, the Archivist Dom Philip Jebb finds nothing of relevance aside from one or two letters from Walter Piper, though no reference to St Walstan in them, nor any sign of the painting. However, Dom Philip writes:

> *Dom Bede was a careful scholar, so I would be surprised if what he wrote in 'Some Norfolk Rood Screens' was inaccurate at the time of writing.*

The Norwich antiquary Walter Piper was a devotee of St Walstan and in the early 1900s wrote several articles concerning his life and cult for the Northamptonshire Diocesan magazine.

REFERENCES:

Some Norfolk Rood Screens Described by Dom Cam Bede (A Supplement to Blomefield's *Norfolk*, 1929)

NORTH BURLINGHAM, St Andrew

S Walstanus is found here on a **16th-century screen painting**. The face is obliterated, crowned and the figure is barefoot with scythe and wearing an ermined gold cape over a red robe. Careful observation shows that St Walstan, in company with some of the other saints, is wearing gold rings on two fingers of his right hand and on the left thumb. The gold purse at the girdle has previously been thought to indicate his charity to the poor, the word 'opifer' on the panel taken to mean 'succourer'. However, if the word is 'opifex', and taken to mean 'worker' or 'artisan', the purse might contain sand for use with a strickle (see Chapter 8 for a discussion on wooden scythe sharpeners). The strickle at the base of the scythe is clear and unambiguous. It even has the circular slot into which the narrow end of the strickle fitted when not in use.

There would appear to be no particular significance in the three shell-like tassels hanging from the purse, though there have been attempts to describe them as scallops and, therefore, a symbol of pilgrimage.

Dated 1536, this is believed to have been the last screen erected in Norfolk before the Reformation.

REFERENCES:

Screen at North Burlingham John Gunn (NNAS Vol 3)

www.uea.ac.uk

NORWICH, All Saints see NORWICH, St Julian

NORWICH, St John the Baptist Catholic Cathedral

Walstan is depicted in one of **six medallions** of East Anglian saints in the North Transept or 'Queens' window. As well as St Walstan, the centre window medallions include SS William, Sigebert, Ethelburga, Ethelbert and Godrick. The window was designed by the Duke of Norfolk and erected by his family in 1909. John Hardman & Co of Birmingham made the windows which, as well as the six East Anglian saints, include the theme of pilgrimage.

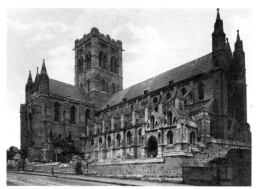

St John's was begun in 1882 and took 28 years to build, the opening ceremony taking place in December 1910.

REFERENCES:

A Great Gothic Fane J W Picton (1913)

Norwich Roman Catholic Cathedral, A Building History Anthony Rossi (1998)

NORWICH, St James (with Pockthorpe)

A redundant church – now the Norwich Puppet Theatre – but the original site of a **16th-century rood screen**, which contained panels of SS Walstan and Blida that are now at St Mary Magdalene (*qv*).

Keyser (1883) wrote:

Rood screen. Destroyed; some of the panels are in private possession with figures of SS Oswald, Sitha, Walstan, Blaise, Blida, Helen, Joan of Valois (with date 1505), Jude, Martin, Simon, Agnes, etc.

REFERENCES:

The History of the Church and Parish of St James with Pockthorpe, Norwich Revd Sidney Long (Graham Cummings, circa 1961)

NORWICH, St Julian

One of the **stone figures** on the stem of the **octagonal Perpendicular font** (dated 1420) is given as 'Wulstan' in the church guide. Unusually, the saint carries a wheatsheaf instead of a scythe as his specific emblem. The font was originally in All Saints' Church, until 1977, when that church became redundant. The living of St Julian's went with All Saints' until 1930. The font is similar in design to that in St Mary Magdalene, where St Blida has been identified as one of the stem figures, and was taken there from St James' with Pockthorpe.

This identification is by no means safe, but the 20th-century tradition of naming the stem figure Wulstan qualifies it for consideration. It is given as Walstan by Mortlock & Roberts.

REFERENCES:

Norfolk Churches: No 2 Norwich, Central and South Norfolk D P Mortlock & C V Roberts (1985)

NORWICH, St Laurence

St Walstan is on a panel of a **20th-century reredos** in this disused church, currently under the care of the Churches Conservation Trust. A field officer for the trust, Roy Tricker, made the identification in 1997. Although not ancient, the three-part reredos, designed by Edwin Tench and made by John Howard in 1921 as the parish's war memorial, contains an arresting and unique painting of Bawburgh Church, picked out in gold. The artist was Mr A Kingston Rudd of Wolferton, who unfortunately died before he was able to complete the entire reredos. As a result the central panels are not painted and other parts appear incomplete.

The 15th-century St Laurence hides its size and grandeur, having been built between St Benedict's Street and Westwick Street on land which falls away towards the River Wensum valley. Part of its construction is below the pavements of St Benedict's, while in Westwick Street it towers above street level, the foundations perching on an eight-foot wall. The reredos is among the few remaining pieces of church furniture left inside.

The Bishop of Thetford dedicated the reredos on 2 June 1921 and it was unveiled by Commandant Bullard, who said:

I unveil this reredos to the glory of God and in memory of the gallant men connected with the parishes of S Laurence with S Gregory who laid down their lives in the Great War.

The reredos comprises three sections. The central panels, which show an angel guarding the Garden of Eden and Melchizedech the Priest-King of Salem, were drawn but not painted. Other scenes appear incomplete, but some, like that of St Walstan, show by the finished sections that the whole would have been a considerable work of art. St Walstan's right hand, for example, is little more than a suggestion and the lighted lantern that he carries is basic in outline and lacks definition.

Rudd seems to have by-passed much of the background and has not completed the figures before succumbing to temptation and embarking on the final gold over-painting of St Walstan's crown and belt fittings, and the truly charming Bawburgh Church picture which is the star of the entire work.

In the southern section, the panel to the right of St Walstan is of St Withburga (sister of St Etheldreda) and she, too, is unfinished, though her halo and crosier are picked out in gold. There is little doubt that the church (to represent Ely Cathedral), which she holds as her specific emblem, would also have been golden had the artist lived.

To St Walstan's left is surely one of the most bizarre portrayals of St Petronilla in Norfolk, if not England. Petronilla, the legendary daughter of St Peter, is shown as a young child, wearing a fur-lined mantle that hangs down over her back. Her dress is short, just touching her knees, and most endearingly draws attention to her blue shoes that are secured by a strap and button, fashionable in the 1920s, over her white ankle socks. She, too, is gilded in parts and we shall never know what treatment Rudd intended for the huge, blue ribbon bow used to tie the neck of her mantle. Her head is strangely disembodied and an adult face wears a rather long-suffering, if somewhat petulant, expression. She carries a single key, given to her by her father, and a book clasped in her right hand.

There is no known record of why SS Walstan, Felix, William and Withburga were chosen for the reredos memorial, other than the obvious deduction that they are all East Anglian saints. Since Petronilla's feast date is 31 May and Walstan's is 30 May, both could have been included to honour the men lost at sea in the Battle of Jutland (31 May 1916).

A curious feature of the St Laurence reredos is in the faces of the saints. They appear so realistic that they are clearly intended as caricatures of real people, living or dead, in the 1920s. In the northern section (immediately below the portrayal of St Laurence being engulfed by fire) is St Felix, the first Bishop of East Anglia, and Roy Tricker points to the surprising likeness of St Felix to Archbishop Randall Thomas Davidson, who was Archbishop of Canterbury at the time. Next to St Felix is St Edmund, who bears a more than passing resemblance to George V. St William of Norwich is dressed in short trousers, long socks and walking shoes. He was perhaps a son, grandson or any contemporary schoolboy known to the artist.

An onlooker is stoking the flames below St Laurence and the artist has endowed the picture with what purports to be classical sculpture behind the scene. It is tempting to imagine that the onlooker, too, was based on someone known to Mr Rudd. It is by no means clear if the artist's intention was to compliment his models; perhaps there are artistic jokes to be discovered, or these are cartoons of prominent politicians or churchmen.

There is no immediate choice of candidates as model for St Walstan, although he could be mistaken for the Revd Gabriel Young, Vicar at Bawburgh from 1892 to 1931. He is featured with an open, kindly face and thus sympathetically portrayed. He carries a lantern to lighten the darkness, his scythe as his specific emblem (although its current state of dilapidation leaves the scythe outline barely discernible), and a painting of the north aspect of Bawburgh Church, where his Shrine Chapel had stood until the Reformation, hangs by a chain from a buckle. The painting is contained on a Bible's front cover, suspended from the ornate waist belt, with part of its right side hidden behind Walstan's cloak. The rounded spine of the Bible can clearly be seen and the first letters 'Ho' and 'Bib' show concern for detail. In his right hand, he carries a peculiar dome-shaped object (possibly intended as his generic emblem of a crown, which resembles the dome of St Paul's Cathedral and is utterly unwearable!), again picked out in gold.

Might at least one of the faces of the reredos portray if not the notorious Father Ignatius himself, then at least some identifiable members of his Order of St Benedict? Or perhaps Bishop Pelham, under whose jurisdiction the church was when Ignatius arrived in Norwich? The Revd Joseph Lyne, 'Father Ignatius' of the Elm Hill community, and his monks used the Church of St Laurence as their place of workshop in the 1850s and on that account it became the centre of protest on more than one occasion. Father Ignatius (who in 1864 led a pilgrimage to St Walstan's Well, amid much public disorder) was a constant irritant to the Honourable John Thomas Pelham, a member of the family of the Earls of Chichester and an old-fashioned Evangelical. Bishop Pelham eventually gave permission for his Norwich clergy to pass the monks over at communion if they presented themselves in their black habits in their churches.

In 1864 Ignatius took exception to the pew rents in St Laurence. The pews were, he told the Revd Edwin Hillyard, Vicar of St Laurence's and supporter of the Third Order, to be removed. Following Hillyard's refusal, Ignatius sent his monks in to rip out the pews and reduce them to firewood, which they succeeded in doing. The parishioners of St Laurence's had given the pews and there was a furious reaction in Norwich to this act of vandalism. While many deplored the practice of pew rents, whereby titled or rich persons could own a pew merely by paying for it, the event brought the Revd Hillyard into disrepute and made the Church of St Laurence notorious for many years afterwards.

The reredos paintings of St Laurence are currently in a dull and grimy state, and suffering from the damp and neglect caused by over thirty years of disuse.

The Churches Conservation Trust has made good the roof and the building is water-tight, but it remains to be seen what will happen to the atmospheric and majestic church of St Laurence.

REFERENCES:

Draft Guide to the Church of St Laurence Roy Tricker (1999)

The Old Churches of Norwich Noel Spencer & Arnold Kent, Revised by Alec Court (Jarrolds, 1990)

St Laurence: Unveiling & Dedication of the War Memorial (Norfolk Studies Library N940 465)

St Walstan at St Lawrence's Betty Martins (Bawburgh News, Vol 15 No 176)

SS Walstan & Blida: List of Norfolk Iconography Carol Twinch (NARG, 2001)

The Reredos at the Church of St Laurence, Norwich Carol Twinch (Church Archaeology, 2003)

NORWICH, St Mary Magdalene

Two **16th-century screen panels**, from a set of ten originally from the Church of St James (with Pockthorpe), contain the unique example of SS Walstan and Blida at the same location. It is the only known extant screen painting of St Blida (see also St Blida gazetteer below). A barefooted St Walstan, with golden halo, wears a green robe and in his right hand holds a wooden staff with a blade tied to its top.

The ten panels belonged to a rood screen thought to date from around 1515 (although some painting was carried out in 1479) and until the early 20th century were in the now redundant Church of St James (with Pockthorpe). Although these surviving panels are free from apparent defacement, they have suffered eccentric restoration in either the late 1800s or early 1900s, and possibly both. Although there is a degree of doubt over the absolute identification of St Blida, there is little doubt that the scythe is original and indicates Walstan.

REFERENCES:

The History of the Church and Parish of St James with Pockthorpe, Norwich Revd Sidney Long (c 1961)

In Search of St Walstan (pp 147-150) Carol Twinch (1995)

SAINT WALSTAN

NORWICH, St Thomas, Heigham Road

Drawings and plans for a **stained glass window** (left), commissioned in 1960, depict St Walstan with Bawburgh's round-towered church at foot, holding the scythe blade in his right hand. The commission was never executed but the design still exists with Kings of Norwich.

SPARHAM, St Mary

St Walstan is found here on a **15th-century panel** with St Thomas of Canterbury. St Walstan is robed, with a crown (to denote royal blood), scythe, and two calves at foot. In his left hand he carries what has traditionally been identified as a sceptre, though it is now thought to be possibly an ornate (and hopelessly impractical!) strickle, its working edge criss-crossed to take the sand and grease mixture. It is likely that the artist was not familiar with the use of a strickle, although he has incorporated an almost perfect example of one at the base of the scythe (see also Chapter 8). He might have been working from an older model and interpreted the sharpener as a sceptre, to match the crown. It is in any case an unwieldy tool and, if indeed it is a sceptre, a wooden one and of inferior quality.

The panel is from the original 15th-century screen and is one of only four remaining. The panels are framed and not *in situ*. Two panels illustrate a rare depiction of the Dance of Death and the other two SS Walstan and Thomas.

REFERENCES:

St Mary's, Sparham M J Sayer (1976) [First edition 1959 by the Revd C L S Linnell]

Painting by Harriet Gunn of
*St Walstan panel at **Sparham.***

(Bishop's Library, Northampton)

TAVERHAM

The **village sign** (left), which stands at the corner of Sandy Lane and the main Fakenham Road, was designed by Harry Carter and given by the Women's Institute in 1970. St Walstan stands in the framework of a circle, the River Wensum and some beech trees as background, wearing a green robe with ermine cape, holding a cross in one hand and a scythe in the other. Apparel is reminiscent of that at Barnham Broom and includes two calves. The beech trees are a reminder of those that, until the 1970s, grew in Beech Avenue and were planted to commemorate the Battle of Trafalgar (1805).

Walstanham Plantation

This is the preferred site for **St Walstan's Well**, in a small copse below Taverham Church. Reputed to be the location of Nalga's farm and Walstan's death.

Norgate writes of a reference to the well in an old lease book as 'laying between Langwongs Furlong on the part of the South and the land of Mary Branthwayt north, and abutting a way leading from Taverham to Crostwick'. This suggests the site somewhere on what is now Breck Farm.

There is also a **St Walstan's Road** in Taverham.

REFERENCES:

An Illustrated History of Taverham T B Norgate (1969 and 1972)

Village Signs Frances Procter and Philippa Miller (1973)

www.taverham-online.co.uk

The restored south aisle window at **Cawston** *contains a fragment of medieval glass bearing the name 'Blida'.*

St Blida

That there was a Norfolk St Blida (Blide, Blythe or Blithe) has been established, but the possibility that she was St Walstan's mother is not yet proven. No mention is made of Blida's sainthood in either the English or Latin Lives of St Walstan, only that she is royal. The English Life says Walstan is 'a kings sonne', therefore his mother 'Blythe' is a queen, while in the Latin Life, Walstan is said to have derived his parentage of 'distinguished royal stock'.

It is not yet certain if St Blida attained sainthood on her own account (and subsequent to that of her son) or if there was confusion between the Norfolk St Blida and Walstan's mother of the same name. No biographical details, nor any feastdate, can be attributed to St Blida and what cult there was ended at the Reformation. She is, however, a saint local to Norfolk and as such earns a place in the county's medieval religious life.

BABINGLEY, St Felix

The **medieval screen** was destroyed by fire in 1854. It contained a number of female saints, listed (in retrospect) by Keyser (1883), who names Blida at Babingley. The old, ruined church is thought to be the site of the first Christian church planted in East Anglia by St Felix, although it has now been derelict for over a century. St Felix landed in Norfolk about 600 AD and established his See at Dunwich.

Dawson Turner made drawings of the screen shortly before the fire, from which identification of St Blida was made (by Husenbeth). However, a good account of the screen is given by Mrs Herbert Jones, in which no mention is made of St Blida.

The modern tin and thatch church of Babingley (built in the 1890s by the Prince of Wales, Edward VII) belongs to Her Majesty the Queen and is located close to the Sandringham Estate. In the 1990s it began to follow its predecessor into decay and for many years was not used for services. However it is now St

Felix Chapel and home to the British Orthodox Community of St Mary & St Felix, part of the Orthodox Church of Egypt.

REFERENCES:

Sandringham, Past & Present Mrs Herbert Jones (Sampson Law, 1883)

www.findachurch.co.uk

CAWSTON, St Agnes

A fragment of **medieval glass** in one of the six **clerestory windows** bears the name 'Blida'. Two teenage boys found the fragments at the Rectory in 1932 and restored them during their holidays. One of the boys went on to be ordained and became the Rural Dean at Aylsham; the other was Dennis King, who became a professional glass expert and founder of Kings of Norwich.

It is this tiny fragment of pre-Reformation glass that makes it impossible to dismiss entirely the possibility of a cult to St Blida.

REFERENCES:

Mediaeval Glass Restored to Cawston Church Revd Christopher Woodforde (NNAS Vol XXV)

St Agnes, Cawston Church Guide (1989)

Cawston, A Short History of a Norfolk Village John Kett (1995)

MARTHAM, St Mary

There is now no evidence in the church of the '**Chapel to St Blide of Martham**' and only sketchy evidence that the south aisle was at one time dedicated to 'St Blide'. Blomefield refers to 'the Chapel of St Blide of Martham' (1479) and to a bequest from Richard Fuller of Norwich, tanner, who gave 10s to the church at Martham 'where St Blide lyeth' (1522).

The present church was rebuilt in 1377 and there appears to be no contemporary reference to St Blide or Blida at that time, suggesting a chapel dedication of a late 15th-century date. Bryant mentioned that there was 'probably' a chapel on the south aisle dedicated to St Blide, Blida or Blythe, who was buried there and said to be the wife of Benedict. A manuscript in the British Museum (cited but not referenced by Bryant) says that Blida's Chapel existed in 1479 and 1506.

REFERENCES:

Blomefield's *Norfolk* (Reg Alabaster Norw. Fol 163).

Bryant (see bibliography)

NORTH TUDDENHAM, St Mary

In 1935, the Revd Christopher Woodforde wrote that St Blida 'was once to be seen in a **chancel window** of North Tuddenham Church'.

M R James had previously (*Suffolk and Norfolk*, 1930) referred to the nave windows at North Tuddenham:

> … *Nelson's book names SS Bartholomew, Blida, Edward Confessor, Edmund, Lawrence, and James the Great. I did not discern all of these.*

It is not clear if St Blida was among those he did discern.

Philip Nelson, however, wrote in 1913:

> *Amongst remains of ancient glass are St Bartholomew, St Blida, St Edward the Confessor, St Edmund, St Laurence, and St James Major, each bearing an emblem.*

Husenbeth's Emblems gives 'a female with apparently the name of St Blida … N Tuddenham – chancel – NE window' and appears to indicate uncertainty. Roeder takes up the theme in 1956 and says that St Blida is 'venerated' at North Tuddenham. However, no safe evidence of St Blida can now be found in the church and the late Dennis King (1912-1995) of Norwich, who worked extensively on the renovation of the North Tuddenham glass, discounted the idea.

REFERENCES:

Medieval Glass Restored to Cawston Church Revd Christopher Woodforde (NNAS, Vol 25, 1935)

The panels of SS Walstan and Blida (right) now at **Norwich St Mary Magdalene** *are the only known example of the two saints at the same location.*

NORWICH, St Mary Magdalene

The only known **screen painting** of St Blida, and a possible **font figure**, are now at St Mary Magdalene, though originally at St James (with Pockthorpe). This is the only extant example of SS Walstan and Blida at the same location. The panels are thought to date from 1515, although some painting was carried out in 1479.

Like St Walstan, Blida wears a green cloak and a halo but holds a book in her left hand and a quill in her right. She is named in the Church Guide as one of the figures on the font stem, which was also removed from St James.

Keyser (1883) names Blida as one of the figures on the St James' roodscreen, said to be in private possession (later discovered to be the Revd James Bulwer).

In addition to their singular qualities, the panels have an extraordinary history. From the 16th to the middle of the 19th century they were in St James', though it is uncertain if they were restored in 1515 to replace an older screen or whether they originated at that time. How they survived the Reformation is also uncertain, but they were still in St James' in 1849 when they were removed from the church as part of some renovation work. In that year Husenbeth made a drawing of the panel of St Walstan, on which he recorded that the panels came from St James' but were then in the possession of the Revd James Bulwer of Hunworth, who was an antiquary and something of an authority on the history of Pockthorpe. Husenbeth also stated that the panels were, at that time, 'all painted over red' and that James Bulwer removed said paint.

Were the panels painted red at the Reformation, perhaps, to save them from destruction? Or, as suggested by the Revd Sidney Long, one-time Vicar of St James' and author of the church history, was the paint applied in the 19th century?

The panels stayed with James Bulwer and over thirty years later, in an 1882 edition of *Emblems*, Husenbeth recorded the panels were still in private possession, although James Bulwer had died in 1879.

By 1896, however, the panels were said by M R James (in *The Life of St William of Norwich*) to be in the possession of Mr J J and Miss Florence

Font at St Mary Magdalene.

Colman. The panel containing St William was photographed for the book around 1896. Apparently the panels had been sold on Norwich Market for a shilling apiece and were purchased by the Colman family, who had them restored in 1917.

In the *Eastern Daily Press* in 1905 ('Walks round Norwich') it was reported:

Visitors to the Loan Exhibition at the recent Church Congress may remember the quaint figure of St Walstan from a panel painting formerly in St James's Church, Norwich, exhibited by Mr J J Colman. Dr Husenbeth notes that the panel in question is 'in private possession at Aylsham'.

How the panels had ended up on Norwich Market remains a mystery, but fortuitously they eventually came into the hands of Russell J Colman, who returned them to St James', where they were placed on the north wall in the Sanctuary. There they remained, undisturbed, for almost thirty years.

In 1946 the panels were again restored, re-sited on the chancel steps and re-dedicated in January 1947 by the Bishop of Norwich.

St James' was declared redundant in 1968 and the congregation moved to St Mary Magdalene in Silver Road. It was decided that the panels and the font should also go to the new church. In 1971 the Revd Malcolm Menin took charge of the panels and in 1974, after again being cleaned and restored, they were finally taken to St Mary Magdalene, where they can now be seen, together with the font.

A fuller description of the panels' history appears in *In Search of St Walstan*.

WORSTEAD, St Mary

St Mary's is said to contain **icons** of both SS Walstan and Blida, and given the huge importance of agriculture to Worstead it would not be surprising to find either saint here.

Husenbeth (*Life of St Walstan*, 1859) writes that the name Blida occurs:

... as the writer lately discovered, in the inscription on the noble rood screen at Worstead, as the name of the wife who, conjointly with her husband, gave the

screen to the Church in 1512: where it appears as Blide uxoris ejus. *The name of Blyth is common in Norfolk, and probably comes from St Blida.*

However, such a dedication cannot now be found. Since no actual site was named, it might be a reference to the now-ruined Chapel of St Andrew.

In 1917, M R James wrote that the name 'Blida' occurs on the **screen**, and in Suffolk and Norfolk writes that drawings of the screen, made in 1832, show a female saint with an attribute, taken to be Blida. Later, though, he writes that the screen (that of 1512) was the work of John Albastyr and his wife, Benedicta. The screen was ('dreadfully' he says) re-painted in 1870, when the identities of several saints were changed.

REFERENCES:

Suffolk and Norfolk M R James (1917)

Chapter 5

Suffolk Gazetteer

EVEN BY THE LATE 1990s there was only one recognised pre-Reformation dedication to St Walstan in Suffolk, that at Earl Stonham. Soon after the discovery of the wall painting in Cavenham, however, it became clear that the cult was more prevalent in Suffolk than previously suspected. The Earl Stonham roof carving, the chapel at Bury St Edmunds, several pre-Reformation will bequests (one of which points to a lost window at Beccles) and the possible wall paintings at Ashby give the cult a new and wider respectability in the county. It seems that the intercession of St Walstan was sought not only throughout Norfolk, but also in pre-Reformation Suffolk.

In 2001 there was a flurry of excitement among Walstan-watchers when Anne Marshall suggested that the late 14th-century wall painting at Gisleham might depict St Walstan. Though it has by no means been conclusively proved one way or the other, and the Gisleham wall painting is not a safe identification, it remains on the 'pending' list!

Since publication of the 1995 gazetteer, the main Suffolk additions are the (possible) wall painting at Gisleham, 15th- and 16th-century will bequests (including the lost window at Beccles) and the modern Orthodox icon at Felixstowe. The will of John Waters the Elder of Beccles is particularly poignant. Having witnessed the traumatic days of the Reformation, he died just a few months before the young King Edward VI, who was succeeded by the Catholic

Queen Mary. Mary would attempt to suppress Protestantism and reinstate the Catholic Faith, yet her sister Elizabeth would turn the tables again and champion the Protestant cause.

Little progress has been made in establishing the reason for 'Blyborow town' (understood to be Blythburgh) being given as Walstan's birthplace in the English Life, or why an ancient window should have been dedicated to him at Walberswick. However, with the increased number of representations now accumulated, it points towards greater importance being attached to St Walstan than was traditionally considered likely. The Abbot of Bury St Edmunds was Patron of the Parish of Beccles and it is starting to appear that St Walstan was associated as much with the monastery there as with the Priory at Norwich. The altar at St Mary's (Bury St Edmunds) together with the Cavenham wall painting, will bequests from Mildenhall and Norton, etc., add up to a small but growing total of pieces in the Suffolk jigsaw.

At Felixstowe can be found the most modern representation; the Orthodox Church of SS Felix & Edmund has an icon of St Walstan that was carried in procession at Bawburgh in 1998. Like Bowthorpe in Norfolk, the Felixstowe icon is unique in being inspired by modern spirituality rather than as a memorial.

Apart from the reference to 'his mother Blythe by name' in the English Life, referring to her as St Walstan's mother (and therefore royal by implication), there is no other known reference to St Blida, Blithe or Blythe in Suffolk. Various parallels have been attempted to link the name with the 'Blyth' in Blythburgh and the geographical Blyth Valley, etc., but with no definitive results.

ASHBY, St Mary

Following a period of restoration between 1880 and 1883, a series of **wall paintings** was recorded as having been 'all covered with a fresh coat of whitewash' (Keyser, 1883). They were said to contain:

(i) Last Judgement

(ii) St Catherine

(iii) St William of Norwich

(iv) History of St Wulstan

In 1990 the late Revd Dr Edward Brooks wrote:

Early in 1973 Mrs Eve Baker, one of the country's foremost conservators of wall paintings … visited Ashby Church … Her report was favourable towards the possibility of finding these murals and in due course a second visit will be made to plan a more detailed examination. There seems to have been little disturbance of the fabric of the church over the past five centuries, so we hope their survival is something waiting to be discovered.

Originally Dr Brooks (historian and Rector of Somerleyton with Ashby from 1969 to 1983) had assigned the depiction to St Wul(f)stan, but later decided to give the matter wider consideration (though the planned second visit is not thought to have been made). The Worcestershire Bishop Wulfstan is rarely depicted in East Anglia (although he is possibly to be found in St Mary's, Bury St Edmunds, *qv*) and, reasoned Dr Brooks, '… although St Wulfstan stood for the Saxon Episcopal excellence against the invading Normans this would not be a valid presentation at the time the murals were painted'.

Additional evidence is to be found in the list of Ashby Records. For almost 30 years, between 1361 and 1390, the Rector was one Simon de Bauburgh, whose Patron was Joan, widow of John de Inglose of Loddon, Norfolk. Since he came from the place where St Walstan's Chapel flourished, Simon de Bauburgh might well have influenced the choice of wall painting in Ashby Church. The accompanying paintings of St William of Norwich were likely to be the choice of the Patron, Joan de Inglose. The Inglose family hailed from Loddon, where a rare 15th-century screen painting depicting St William of Norwich can still be seen in the church.

In *St William of Norwich*, Jessop & James wrote:

The church of Ashby had once a series of frescoes, now whitewashed over, one of which is said to have represented St William. It is not, however, now possible to obtain any copy or detailed description of this painting.

The information originates with Keyser.

It is interesting that, instead of the usual single representation of a saint or apostle, the Loddon screen shows complete scenes and Keyser also refers to 'a series' of paintings at Ashby rather than individual ones. If these paintings portray Walstan during his lifetime, they could be unique in showing him as a farm worker rather than a crowned saint. In her assessment of the Cavenham wall painting, Miriam Gill dismisses the possibility that it is intended to portray a scene from Walstan's life as he would need to be shown as a barefoot peasant and only a posthumous image would include the crown and scythe combination.

The possibility of finding St Walstan at Ashby is heightened in the light of a possible identification of St Walstan in medieval wall paintings at Gisleham, only a few miles south. The parishes of Ashby and Gisleham are both in the Diocese of Norwich and the Archdeaconry of Suffolk.

REFERENCES:

List of Buildings in Great Britain having Mural and Other Painted Decorations C E Keyser (1883)

St William of Norwich A Jessop & M R James (1896)

The Popular Guide to Norfolk Churches D P Mortlock & C V Roberts (1985)

A Thousand Years of Village History, Ashby, Suffolk Revd Dr Edward C Brooks (Ash Trust, 1990)

BECCLES, St Michael

In the **will** of John Waters the Elder of Beccles, dated 28 May 1547, he desires to be buried in the churchyard near the **window of 'St Walston'** (see also Chapter 10). Since the churchyard surrounds the church it is not now possible to say which part of it was near St Walstan's window, but was unlikely to be the south-east corner as there were contemporary building operations being carried out to construct the church tower. It was completed hurriedly a couple of years later, in 1550 or thereabouts, at a time when the Dissolution was in progress and it was feared the building money would be taken in tax or merely appropriated by the profligate Henry VIII. John Waters would have lived through the traumatic days of the Reformation and by his reference to 'St Walston' may have been indicating how he felt about it.

It is unlikely that either the west or east windows of St Michael's would have contained St Walstan, since this would have meant a larger devotion or following than is considered likely. There appears to have been no gild to St Walstan which would raise his importance in the town, and – to date – only the will of John Waters to indicate that the window existed. It was probably one of the nave windows, which in itself would lend it a certain status.

The church of St Michael dates from around 1369 (with later additions in the 1450s) so the likely date for the St Walstan window is the second half of the 14th century (which would coincide with the height of his cult). It is possible that further information will come to light on the Beccles window and that other bequests might establish the size and strength of devotion that St Walstan evoked in the town.

This reference to St Walstan is rare in that it postdates the Reformation. Although Peter Northeast points out that it would appear to have no significance beyond showing that the window was still there, it is of considerable interest in raising the existence of a medieval window dedication at Beccles. Unfortunately Beccles suffered many fires in medieval times, and a later one on St Andrew's Eve, 29 November 1586 that destroyed much of the town centre and completely gutted the church. Little survives from the years prior to that except a memorial to John Rede, a former Mayor of Norwich, who died in 1502 and whose tomb is still in the church (though not in its original site and vandalised to make it fit its new place). However, even if the window did not perish in the fire it was unlikely to have survived the visit of William Dowsing on 6 April 1643. His list of offending items at Beccles included 'many superstitious pictures, about 40', which were destroyed.

REFERENCES:

The Parish Church of St Michael the Archangel, Beccles (4th Edition, 1998)

Beccles Revealed Beccles Society (1998)

Blythburgh Church – was St Walstan born near here?

BLYTHBURGH

Named in the 1658 English Life as the **birthplace** of Walstan:

In Blyborow town ye child borne was: his father Benet, his mother Blythe
by name.

However, no other evidence is forthcoming and no mention of Walstan, Blida or Benedict (Benet) can be found in the church or documents relating to Blythburgh.

In 1917, M R James pointed to the principal difference between the Latin Life and the English Life in that '[the English Life] is certainly better here in saying that he was born in Blythburgh in Suffolk'. Quite why he thought so he omitted to explain.

Peter Warner explores the royal connections of Blythburgh in the 10th and 11th centuries, but makes only a passing reference to St Walstan and comes to no firm conclusions.

Walberswick (see below) is a contiguous parish to Blythburgh and their ecclesiastic history runs parallel, but although there is mention of St Walstan at Walberswick, nothing specific to St Walstan at Blythburgh has yet come to light.

REFERENCES:

MS Lambeth 935 (Item 8) *The English Life of St Walston*

Lives of St Walstan M R James (1917)

The Origins of Suffolk Peter Warner (1996)

A Blyth Valley Saint Tony Norton (Blyth Valley Team 'Times', 1999)

Blyth Valley History Note 26 (March, 2000)

BURY ST EDMUNDS, Assumption of the Blessed Virgin Mary

On the **north side** of the West Door is **St Wolston's Chapel**, completed in 1433. Until 1874 the Archdeacon of Sudbury held his visitations and consistory courts in the chapel. As well as the ecclesiastical courts and visitations, it was customary to distribute the gifts of bread to the poor from the chapel, which was

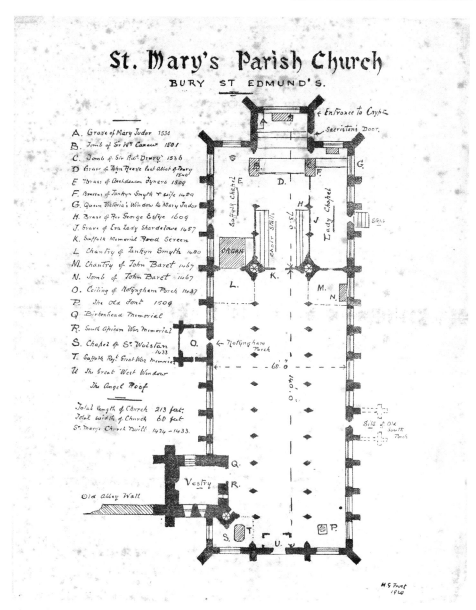

*Plan of St Mary's, **Bury St Edmunds**, showing the location of 'The Chapel of St Wolstan' ('S') built in 1433 (H G Frost, 1920).*

historically separated from the nave by a screen corresponding in character to that which is still visible in the choir. In the chapel, also, executors of wills were required to deliver accounts of their trust.

A Victorian brass plaque that declared the chapel for 'St Wolston, Patron of East Anglian Farmers' was removed some years ago and is now lost. A plan of the church showing the chapel once hung in the nave, but has now also been removed.

The chapel was completed in the 1430s, but as yet no evidence has emerged that might prove it replaced an earlier St Wolston's Chapel in a previous church on the same site. The older church, though, was built by the Benedictines, an order known to favour and champion the cult, and the spelling of Wolston (with two o's instead of a's) might be significant in linking it with the Benedictine English Life, which also employs the 'o' spelling. Interestingly, the spelling 'Walston' also occurs in at least one pre-Reformation Suffolk will (Gislingham, see Chapter 10).

Supplementary evidence of the chapel's dedication derives, as it often does, from contemporary wills and bequests. Thus, in 1503, the chapel is acknowledged by one Sir William Gardiner, priest of the rood altar in the monastery of St Edmund, and cited by the 19th-century editor and antiquary Samuel Tymms in the numerous editions of *The History of St Mary's*. In his will, Sir William bequeathed to the altar of 'saynt Walston in the church of saynt Mary':

> … j masse books & j peyre chalices of sylu & a vestment of blewe sarsenett, a corporas case wt a corp'as in hitt, ij aught clothys; je aught' cloth of sylke wt a frontell to the same; an aught' cloth for the ou parte of the aught' of the sute be for namyd.

A corp'as or corporas denotes a consecrated linen cloth, folded and placed on the altar, beneath the sacred vessels, during the service of Mass. (See also Chapter 10)

In St Wolston's Chapel is the war memorial to the officers and men of the Suffolk Regiment who fell in the First World War, which was unveiled in March

1920. The Book of the Dead contains more than 7000 names. Two of the Colours which flank the monument, those of the 7th and 12th Battalions, were dedicated in October 1920 and those of the 5th Battalion a year later. This cenotaph is considered one of the finest war memorials in England and was designed by W A Tite of London. The material is of alabaster with a base of Ashburton marble.

REFERENCES:

MS Pye: IC 500/2/4/129 (Bury St Edmunds Record Office)

St Mary's Church, Bury St Edmunds Samuel Tymms (1845)

Handbook of Bury St Edmunds Samuel Tymms (various editions)

St Mary's Parish Church HB Gray (1920)

St Mary's, Bury St Edmunds Clive Paine (1986)

CAVENHAM, St Andrew

Here, on the **north wall** of the aisle-less nave, is the only extant **medieval wall painting** of St Walstan, dated at between 1465-1485. It was discovered in 1967 but for twenty years remained unidentified until finally authenticated by Dr David Park of the Courtauld Institute of Art in the early 1990s. The painting dates from the latter half of the 15th century and has considerable underdrawing. It measures approximately two feet by two feet eight inches and shows Walstan crowned, holding a scythe in his left hand and a sceptre in his right hand. Two (or possibly three) small figures are at his feet looking up at him.

Walstan's scythe and crown are clearly defined, and although the 'sceptre' has been authenticated as such, its original design and purpose is open for discussion (see Chapter 8).

The significance or identity of the small figures at Walstan's feet remains a mystery. They were originally thought to be two adult figures, but on closer

*This medieval depiction at **Cavenham** is unique in being the only extant wall painting of St Walstan.*

examination a smaller figure emerges between the two, indicating parents and child. It is not clear if they portray 15th-century donors of the painting, representative pilgrims, or whether they are the Taverham farmer and his wife of the Walstan legend. Another possibility is that they are Blida and Benedict, showing Walstan as a child. However, writing in 1995, Miriam Gill suggests that the size of the figures, i.e. about a third the size of St Walstan himself, suggests that the couple are devotees, and:

> The most obvious objection to a narrative reading [of the couple] is the fact that Walstan is depicted as a king. An image of Walstan during his life would need to show a barefoot peasant; only a 'posthumous' ideal image, like those on the rood screens, could show him as befitted his rank.

The couple are, then, more likely to be the donors of the painting than either the Taverham couple or Walstan's parents.

The identification of St Walstan in a wall painting only seven miles north-west of Bury St Edmunds and on the Icknield Way, an ancient pilgrim route, is considered significant in defining the extent of the cult of St Walstan.

It is also the only known representation in the Diocese of Ely, although a Mildenhall will bequest of 1485 does mention St Walstan. Thomas Fuller of Mildenhall wished for a pilgrim to go to seven places, including one to 'St Walstan', but nothing more.

REFERENCES:

St Andrew's Church, Cavenham, Suffolk: Brief History and Guide Roy Tricker (1982)

The Saint with a Scythe Miriam Gill (The Suffolk Institute of Archaeology & History, Vol XXXVIII, 1995)

Community to Decide Historic Church's Fate (East Anglian Daily Times, 2 May 1998)

Under-threat church has rare painting (East Anglian Daily Times, 12 May 1998)

Meeting to save Church (East Anglian Daily Times, 29 August 1998)

www.cavenham22.freeserve.co.uk

EARL STONHAM, St Mary the Virgin

In the magnificent **single hammer-beamed roof** are 22 canopied niches, each containing a **carved figure** – one of which is St Walstan (ninth figure on the south side of the nave). The roof is made of chestnut and dates from 1460. Binoculars are required, though, as St Walstan stands way up on one of the wall posts which in turn rest on wooden corbels that are carved with grotesques. He stands between St Catherine (sword in hand and a broken wheel at her feet) and St Osmond (Book of the Sarum Use in hand).

The scythe blade is uppermost below its staff, in the working position, and the strickle is (apparently) in transport mode. Given the position of St Walstan's right hand it is likely that he was carrying a strickle, sceptre, crown or other emblem (see also Chapter 8). Since the carving was beheaded in the 1640s there is no evidence that the figure was crowned.

Members of the Suffolk Institute visited St Mary's on 11 July 1871 'amid pouring rain, which continued more or less throughout the day'. The Rector, the Revd J Castley, read an account of the church, observing 'St Walstan, with a scythe in his left hand'.

All the figures are minus their heads, the vandalism having always been attributed to William Dowsing, or one of his agents, carried out in the 1640s. However, there is no specific mention of destruction at Earl Stonham (or Stonham Earl) in Dowsing's *Journal*, although there are churchwardens' accounts which record replacement of clear glass in 1643, thus indicating that the iconoclasts had been at work. Neighbouring Stonham Aspall was targeted in 1644-45 by Edmund Blomfield, a churchwarden at St Mary's, a member of the local and staunchly Puritan Blomfield family. (See *The Journal of William Dowsing* for a full and detailed discussion of iconoclasm in East Anglia during the English Civil War.)

REFERENCES:

Stonham Earl Meeting and Excursion 1871 (Suffolk Institute of Archaeological Proceedings, Vol V 1886)

The Church of St Mary the Virgin, Earl Stonham 'F R' (1962)

FELIXSTOWE, St Felix & St Edmund Orthodox Church

Established in 1997, this foundation of the Orthodox Church has become the centre for English-speaking Orthodox of all backgrounds. Among the **icons** commissioned by the church is that of **'St Walstan of Taverham'**, which was prepared for the occasion and carried in procession at the first Orthodox Pilgrimage to Bawburgh in June 1998. The icon was hand-painted in the traditional style of the Orthodox Church at the Walsingham studio of the artist Leon Liddament. It is painted in the traditional style of the Orthodox Church.

Icon of St Walstan at the Orthodox Pilgrimage to Bawburgh in 1998.

REFERENCES:

The Iconography of Leon Liddament John Henshall (Suffolk & Norfolk Life, June, 2000)

Felixstowe Orthodox Church: www.odox.net

FRITTON, St Edmund

In Suffolk until 1974 when it was moved to Norfolk (*qv*).

GISLEHAM, Holy Trinity

In 2001 St Walstan was suggested as the subject of a **medieval wall painting** contained in a window-splay on the unusually wide north wall. The late 14th- or early 15th-century wall paintings were conserved in 1992 and are of high quality.

In 2001 Anne Marshall wrote:

Each [painting] is in a window-splay on the north wall of the church, with an empty splay where paintings may once have been facing each other. The painting at the left has a female figure, with loose hair, a crown and a very large halo, which seems to be looking down from heaven on a figure below. There is a strong likelihood that this is the Virgin Mary, but there are other candidates. Great shafts of light radiate down from the stylised clouds below the saint, framing the head of a crowned male figure. The most significant detail is the object he holds in his right hand, which looks like a scythe or sickle. If this is so, then he is very likely to be St Walstan of Bawburgh.

The paintings in the second window show the Annunciation: the Archangel Gabriel looks down on the Virgin who wears a rose-wreath on her head. (The identification of the female figure as the Virgin is by no means secure and a possible alternative of St Dorothy has been suggested.)

However, in 2003, Anne Marshall cast doubt on her original identification:

I still cannot identify these mysterious paintings with absolute certainty … it should be stressed that Walstan is still a possibility, but revision and minute scrutiny of all the available photographs has suggested another candidate, and I now suspect that this might in fact be St Edmund of East Anglia, holding several arrows. If this is true, then the 'scythe or sickle' previously suggested is nothing of the kind, and might be, rather, part of a looping scroll with a long-vanished inscription, which once curved around the saint's arm and continued lower down his torso. Or it might even simply be the border of his cloak.

Such discussions serve to emphasise the ease with which this saint would have been immediately identified when the scythe, or looping scroll, was as visible as they once were to the parishioners and visiting pilgrims of pre-Reformation Suffolk. (An update on further pronouncements by Anne Marshall can be found on the 'Painted Church' website.)

If safe identification at this site is made, it improves the case for Ashby, only a few miles north of Gisleham and one of the many churches on at least one of

*Medieval wall painting at **Gisleham** – is it St Walstan or St Edmund?*

the many pilgrim routes to and from the East Coast ports. Indications are that the Gisleham paintings were executed by French or Flemish painters whose work has been identified in other parts of Suffolk (the right hand splay painting of the Archangel Gabriel bears a striking resemblance to the screen paintings of St Walstan at Sparham).

What significance, if any, is to be derived from the evidence of a medieval window to St Walstan at Beccles, only a few miles to the west of Gisleham?

Like Ashby, Gisleham is in the Diocese of Norwich and the Archdeaconry of Suffolk. Also similar to Ashby is the secondary, or supporting, evidence found in the Parish Rectors. Early Rectors at Gisleham include one John of Martham, who has no attributed dates but is sandwiched between John of Hemmesby (1330) and Elais of Hoxne (1339). Matching John of Martham's dates to around the 1330s, might he have brought a following of St Walstan from his native Martham, where the cult of St Blida was strong enough to inspire a chapel in her name? The possibility that St Walstan was also venerated at Martham is supported by mention of the screen painting (see St Mary's, Martham in the Norfolk Gazetteer).

By the same token, might the identity of the unknown female saint in the neighbouring window arch be St Blida?

This is, however, amateur speculation and undoubtedly leaves a gap between John of Martham's 1330s rectorship and the 'late 14th-century' description of the wall painting (although it might be only a gap of one generation). It also ignores the fact that Elais of Hoxne hailed from a village on the Suffolk-Norfolk border that is a contender for the place of St Edmund's martyrdom and a site very strongly associated with that saint.

REFERENCES:

The Church of the Holy Trinity, Gisleham (2000)

Medieval Paintings of St Walstan of Bawburgh, Gisleham Anne Marshall 2001

www.paintedchurch.org

GISLINGHAM

In 1493, John More of Gislingham named the **shrine of 'saynte Walston'** in his will (see also Chapter 10). More was giving instructions for the completion of pilgrimages that he had vowed to do in his lifetime, and so morally bound to do, even after death. The list (by courtesy of Peter Northeast) is:

Our Lady of Walsingham

St Walston

Our Lady of Owtyng (Essex)

St Nicholas of Thebenham (Tibbenham, Norfolk)

Our Lady of Woolpit

St Margaret (almost certainly of Easton Bavents)

The Blessed Rood of Gislingham

Good King Henry (Windsor)

It is not entirely clear where 'Owtyng' is (other than in Essex) but Peter Northeast suggests that it could be Roding (pronounced 'Roothing'), which also occurs as 'Ooting'.

REFERENCES:

Hervye (folio 442)

KENTON

In the will of Nicholas Wade of Kenton (1508) he requests **pilgrimages** to be done by a priest to Our Lady of Walsingham, to the good rood of Beccles and to St Walstan at Bawburgh. A mass was to be sung at each. (See also Chapter 10)

MILDENHALL

St Walstan is mentioned in the will of Thomas Fuller of Mildenhall (1485), who wished for a **pilgrim** to go to seven places, including one to 'St Walstan'. (See also Chapter 10)

NORTON

In the will of John Billynge of Norton (1526) he requests a **pilgrimage** to Our Lady of Walsingham and 'St Walston'. (See also Chapter 10)

RUMBURGH

In the 15th century the Prior of the monks at Rumburgh had a portion of the tithes incumbent on the church of St Mary and St Walstan at Bawburgh. Valued at two marks, it was held by grant of the Abbot of St Mary's (York) to which Rumburgh was a cell. York Abbey had acquired it as a gift of the Earl of Britain, it being part of the tithes of the property of that Earl in Bawburgh. However, in 1525 Dr Stephen Gardiner, secretary to Cardinal Thomas Wolsey, visited the priory and in 1528 York Abbey released their revenues from Rumburgh (and therefore Bawburgh) to the Cardinal's new St Peter's College at Ipswich. (The college had a very short life. Wolsey suppressed several small priories in Suffolk during 1526 and 1527 to make way for his new college but it was dismantled after his death in 1530.)

It may be that the Rumburgh parishioners were aware of St Walstan, given that it would have been in the interests of the Prior to encourage devotion to the Norfolk shrine (in order to increase the shrine revenues).

REFERENCES:

Blomefield's *Norfolk*

Rumburgh Remembered: Church and Village Caroline Cardwell

WALBERSWICK, St Andrew

The reference to the **lost window of 'St Wolstane'** comes from Thomas Gardner, who in 1754 wrote:

The windows of St Christopher and St Wolstane seem to have been taken from this [the old church] and set up in the latter Church, where all the Images, with

The old church at Walberswick was the site for a pre-Reformation window to 'St Wolstane'.

the Tables of Saint George and King Harry, accompanied them.

The old church, says the Church Guide '... stood on the border of the marshes some three or four hundred yards to the south of the site of the present Church', the last remains of which were finally destroyed in 1728. The move away from the marsh site to the new building took place in 1473, though it seems to have been some twenty years between the dismantling of the old marsh church and the completion of the new one. It was to this new church that the windows of St Christopher and St Wolstane were removed.

Gardner gives no more detail other than an extract from the churchwarden's receipts for 1487. An amount of 8s 4d was paid 'for mendying Seynt Krysteferys Wyndown' while a lesser sum of 9d was 'for mendying Seynt Walsteneys Wyndown'. Both windows have long since been destroyed. The present church of St Andrew has the remaining fragments of 14th- and 15th-century glass, discovered in the 1930s, incorporated into one light of a window in the south wall. They are tiny, unmarked fragments of coloured glass, which give nothing away.

Local historian Merle Tidey named this Wolstane as 'St Wulstan, the Ploughman's Saint', and there would seem to be no reason for thinking that 'Seynt Walsteney' was not St Walstan. What, if any, connection this has with the claim that nearby Blythburgh was Walstan's birthplace has yet to emerge.

To date, specific mention of St Walstan in pre-Reformation glass is unique to Suffolk (i.e. Walberswick and Beccles).

REFERENCES:

In and Around the Village of Walberswick Merle Tidey (1987)

St Andrew's, Walberswick, History of the Church (1988)

An Historical Account of Dunwich, Blithburgh, Southwold with remarks on some places contiguous thereto Thomas Gardner (1754)

In Search of St Walstan (pp 131-133) Carol Twinch (1995)

Blyth Valley Saint Tony Norton (Blyth Valley Team 'Times', July 1999)

The Poaching Priors of Blythburgh, ed. Alan Mackley (2001)

*St Walstan in a 20th-century stained glass window at **Bledlow** in Buckinghamshire.*

Chapter 6

Miscellaneous Gazetteer

A FEATURE OF THE MODERN representations of St Walstan is the use of his image in 20th century glass beyond the boundaries of Essex, Suffolk and Norfolk. In 1947 a church window at Cowden took St Walstan to Kent for the first time, and in 1949 the Wooster family of Buckinghamshire commissioned his image in that county.

The Kent and Buckinghamshire windows were 'discovered' on the internet, and it is possible that others will come to light in due course.

St Walstan's Church in Rongai (Kenya) continues to flourish though – as everywhere – the community is constantly in need of funds for renovation and fabric maintenance.

Pre-Reformation iconography outside East Anglia depends entirely on Gresford.

BUCKINGHAMSHIRE
BLEDLOW, Holy Trinity
In the **north wall** of the chancel, the **St Walstan window** shows him crowned holding a scythe and with a wheatsheaf at his feet in **20th-century stained glass**. He wears a red cloak and green tunic with yellow leggings. There is an inexplicable arrangement of what looks like a rectangular-buckled belt hanging

from the cloak clasp and the figure appears to be raising his tunic provocatively above his left knee!

Barton, Kinder & Alderson, of Brighton (Sussex), made the light in 1949. In the bottom right (green) pane (above the inscription) is found the maker's mark – a monk scribe seated at his lectern (pictured right).

The dedication reads:

This window is placed by Lilian Matilda Wooster in memory of the Wooster family, April 1949.

It is the only known representation of St Walstan in Buckinghamshire. Originally Mrs Lilian Wooster had petitioned to have the window in memory of her husband, Thomas W Wooster, but somewhere along the line it became 'in memory of the Wooster family'. The window cost £83.

The Woosters were a farming family with land at Bledlow, Bledlow Ridge and Princes Risborough. As there were earlier Woosters named Albert it is tempting to think that PG Wodehouse might have got the inspiration for his character 'Bertie Wooster' from the family. However a Mr GLC Wooster wrote to PG Wodehouse and received a personal reply from him on 20 May 1962. PG Wodehouse said that he could not remember how he had got the name Wooster but it may have been from a serial in the old '*Captain*' publication.

In a Preface to a 1970 edition of *Something Fresh* (first published in 1915), PG Wodehouse admitted to basing at least one of his characters on 'living originals'. So far as those researching the Wooster family history can tell, no member of the family was known to Wodehouse, and it is questionable that 'Bertie Wooster' was a living original from Bledlow, though the author did take place and person names from life.

Bledlow is the most western of the Buckinghamshire villages that cluster on the northern spur of the Chilterns and the church lies in a particularly rural corner of the parish. Its picturesque nature has caused it to be used as a location for the television series, *Midsomer Murders*, by Caroline Graham (and starring

John Nettles). Due to the efforts of the Red Kite Reintroduction Programme in the East Midlands, numerous pairs of the graceful Red Kite hover and glide over Bledlow and Bledlow Ridge, drifting low over the countryside, its two-metre wing-span and long forked reddish tail a sight to behold.

REFERENCES:

Welcome to Holy Trinity Church, Bledlow (1998)

Bawburgh News (Vol 20, May 2003)

www.buckscc.gov.uk/glass/images/668-19A.JPG

CLWYD (formerly Denbighshire)
GRESFORD, All Saints

At least three authoritative sources refer to a **pre-Reformation stone figure**, crowned and holding a scythe, at the top of Gresford Church. Of these, the earliest is Bryant (*Norfolk Churches*, 1905), who describes St Walstan as being at Gresford 'crowned, holding a scythe'.

Drake (*Saints and Their Emblems*, 1916) repeats the information, as does M R James in 1917, although his reference was more sceptical:

> *[A] stone figure, crowned and holding a scythe, at the top of Gressford Church, Denbighshire, a place to which I can hardly believe that the fame of St Walstan ever penetrated. The scythe would suit several Western saints: Sativola, Urith, and Kyneburga of Gloucester.*

Gresford historian Dr Colin Jones has found no reference to St Walstan in the village or church archives. The closest reference to the figures comes with a bequest by John Leach, in 1582, who left ten shillings '… towards the erecting of the pynnacles'. Between the eight pinnacles are the same number of figures, carved in front only with the backs left plain. They have, records Bethan Jones, been variously described as kings, knights, evangelists and pilgrims. However, the roof of Gresford Church is exposed to wind and rain and the pinnacles themselves have crashed through the roof on at least five occasions.

*20th-century
stained glass
window at
Cowden in Kent.*

Inside Gresford Church SS Sytha, James (as a pilgrim to Compostela) and Leonard (complete with chains) are found on the 13th-century font, together with Edward the Confessor, the Madonna and Child and angels, but nothing that would represent St Walstan.

Gresford was the first site outside Norfolk to appear in a gazetteer of St Walstan representations but it has never been authenticated and it is difficult to know who first started the rumour and why.

REFERENCES:

A Guide Book to the Parish Church of All Saints, Gresford Bethan Jones (1995)

Gresford Village and Church, and Royal Marford J Collin Jones (1995)

KENT
COWDEN, St Mary Magdalene

Here in **modern stained glass**, given to the parish in 1947, is the only known representation of St Walstan in Kent.

The two-light window (in the **nave south wall**) was designed by H Warren Wilson and carries the inscription:

In heartfelt thanks to God and to His everlasting Glory. This window, the gift of members of this Church, commemorates the remarkable preservation of this village during the years 1939-45.

In the left-hand light, beneath the arms of the See of Canterbury, women are represented by St Bridget, sailors by St Nicholas and '… farmers by St Walstan (Bishop of Worcester 1062-95, canonised 1203)'.

In the right-hand light are the arms of the Diocese of Rochester, St George (for soldiers and airmen), while St Mary Magdalene, as patron saint, holds the church in her hand.

Wartime agriculture is represented by a Land Girl, a member of the Women's

Land Army, and a horse and horseman, in company with the villagers of Cowden, the National Services and a representative family.

The figure of St Walstan – which has a pink halo – holds a cross and his two calves (excellently portrayed though modern in appearance) at his feet. Unfortunately, in the church guide the account is a mixture between St Walstan and Bishop Wulfstan (died 1095 and canonised in 1203). Wulfstan, however, was born of Anglo-Saxon parents at Itchington (Warwickshire) and educated at Evesham and Peterborough abbeys before becoming a priest. He joined the Benedictines at Worcester Cathedral Priory and became Bishop of Worcester in 1062. He governed so wisely that he was the only English bishop retaining his see after the Conquest. His episcopate lasted thirty-two years, during which time he rebuilt the cathedral, and he died while engaged in his daily practice of washing the feet of twelve poor men. None of this could be confused with the Life of St Walstan.

[Another site where a likely mistake is made between Wulfstan and Walstan is at St Mary's, Bury St Edmunds, where the roof figure is said by Tymms to be Walstan, but appears to be a Bishop and therefore more likely to be Wulfstan. Also the identification at St Julian's in Norwich is by no means safe.]

Clearly, though, at Cowden there is no question whatsoever that the figure is intended to be St Walstan and not Bishop Wulfstan.

REFERENCES:

The Parish Church of St Mary Magdalene, Cowden (various editions)

The other Kent connection with the cult of St Walstan is **Miracle 8 of The English Life**:

In Canterbury a crafty man dwelled full right
A weaver and lived by his occupation
Sore vexed with bone ache both day and night.
Specially of his leg, and judged by estimation
That never to be restored to his operation,

Supported by crutches goeth, Holy Thomas to pray
And so continueth long and many a day.

This pain continued, and would not cease.
It hap'd a pilgrim of this country
St Thomas to visit his vow to release.
This lame man doth behold: to him goeth he,
'Man' he saith, 'God comfort thee',
And asketh the cause of his grievance.
'I am visited' he saith, 'after God's pleasance.'

The cause briefly declared, the pilgrim said
'To Holy Walston labour with all thy might,
'Thou shalt in that place of God by him have aid,
'And thy lame leg shall be made full right
'Go thou forward on this night
'A leg of wax offer thou also,
'Thou shalt have health ere thou go.'

This man in his heart avowed anon,
To come to that place wheresoever it is,
Where the body lieth of holy Walston,
He had not gone far from thence I wys
But the pain did slack out of his limbs,
His staves he laid aside then,
To the city of Norwich the way he went.

A leg of wax he did make there
According to his counsel aforesaid,
In his arm he did it bear
To the town Bawburgh and there it laid
Before St Walston, and heartily prayed
Many folks being when he did depart
Both leg and body hale and quarter.

This appears to be a determined effort on the part of the Bawburgh Shrine-keepers to show that St Walstan could, on this occasion at least, outshine St Thomas of Canterbury. Unable to gain the intercession of St Thomas, the weaver is advised to seek St Walstan instead. Happily he had better luck at Bawburgh, where he was duly cured and returned home 'both leg and body hale and quarter'.

REFERENCES:

The English Life (Miracle 8) MS Lambeth 935

ENGLISH CATHEDRAL

An unidentified icon of St Walstan on an **English cathedral** is reputed to have been the inspiration for the dedication of St Walstan's Church in Rongai. An image of **St Walstan (holding a wheatsheaf)** is said to be above an entrance door to an English cathedral.

It is apparent from part of an undated letter sent to Fr Husenbeth that he had instigated enquiries about a dedication in Ely Cathedral, as well as one in London. The letter-writer reports back, saying: '… I have made enquiries about the Church in London, and about the Chapel at Ely, but so far have …'; the rest of the letter, and the identity of the writer, is lost.

So far, no church dedication to St Walstan has been discovered in London, although there is a Wulfstan Street in West London.

However, research in 1994 about a dedication in Ely Cathedral revealed that Keyser (1883) named 'W'lstan' there, but the Dean & Chapter archivist thinks this is likely to refer to the wall paintings, now destroyed, which included Wulfstan, Archbishop of York (d 1023).

REFERENCES:

Husenbeth private papers in Bishop's Library, Northampton

NORTHAMPTON
Bishop's Library

In 1849 Fr Husenbeth instigated a series of the (then known) six documented pre-Reformation paintings of St Walstan for inclusion in *The Life of St Walstan, Confessor*, but they were not used. On the final page he writes:

> *It would have been desirable, and would have accorded with (the author's) anxious wish, to introduce them as illustrations into this little volume. But the expense of doing so would have so far increased the price of the book, as to place it beyond the means of many, who would be anxious to possess it, and might peruse it with interest and edification.*

The **five original paintings** are retained in the Bishop's Library in Northampton and depict the screen paintings at:

(1) Sparham (by 'Mrs Harriet Gunn').

(2) Ludham (by Harriet Gunn, dated 1846).

(3) Barnham Broom (by Husenbeth, dated 10 May 1850).

(4) Formerly in St James Church, Norwich but 'now in the possession of Rev James Bulwer, Aylsham (crossed out and Hamworth substituted) near Thetford' (by Husenbeth, dated 1849). This panel is now at St Mary Magdalene, Norwich.

(5) North Burlingham (by Harriet Gunn).

Harriet (née Turner) Gunn was the wife of the antiquary Revd John Gunn of Irstead, Norfolk. Her father was the botanist and antiquary of Great Yarmouth, Dawson Turner and her mother, Mary Palgrave, came from that distinguished Norfolk family of historians and antiquaries.

References

The Life of St Walstan Husenbeth

Husenbeth private papers in Bishop's Library, Northampton

NORTHUMBRIA

Holy Island of Lindisfarne

The Revd Ray Simpson has a **modern wooden figure** of St Walstan on Holy Island at the Community of Aidan & Hilda (see also Bowthorpe, Chapter 4).

OXFORD

Bodleian Library

In 2000, Professor Nigel Morgan discovered an inscription to St Walstan in a **15th-century psalter** in the Bodleian Library. The hand-held psalter, its pages ruled with two-inch margins, ended up in the possession of a Norfolk family, but there is nothing to denote its original owner.

Professor Morgan writes:

The date of this Psalter is c 1450-75, but these Norfolk saint entries are added, and therefore probably postdate 1475. Walstan on May 30th is described as king and confessor.

The main body of the psalter is the set text of the psalms with six leaves carrying a page for each month and left blank for the owner to write in his or her special saint days. The figure of the first of each month is inscribed with red and ornate script. St Walstan shares 30 May with St Petronilla (although her Feast Day is 31 May).

Investigations continue into the possibility of 'Regina B??da', entered on 7 September, referring to Queen Blida (though Nigel Morgan points out that it should be in the genitive, so is more likely to be Blide). However, 7 September is the feastdate of the rarely depicted St Regina, though why she should turn up in a Norfolk psalter has yet to be discovered and explained.

The psalter once belonged to the Blakeney family, and on 20 August is added the obit (death date) of John Blakeney armiger (a person of high status, entitled to bear arms). John Blakeney probably belonged to the Blakeney family of Sparham (where St Walstan was included on the rood screen), although a

Thomas Blakeney was at Horford Hall Manor, Honingham in 1507, where his descendant John Blakeney was also in 1546 (see Blomefield).

Later the psalter passed into the possession of the Bassingham family, with the names of Francis and Roger Bassingham as owners written in late 15th/early 16th-century script. (A Roger Bassingham was born in 1569 and christened at St Andrew's in Norwich.)

REFERENCES:

MS Rawlinson G20

Information provided by Professor Nigel Morgan

KENYA

RONGAI, St Walstan

The **Church of St Walstan** was built in the early 1950s by settlers and dedicated in 1955 by Bishop Leonard Beecher and Gordon Mayo, Vicar of Nakuru. In 1986 more work took place and a vestry was added, and two years later electricity was installed.

During 1988 St Walstan's Church Hall was dedicated by the Bishop the Rt Reverend Stephen Mwangi. The church is the headquarters of the parish and has nine affiliated churches.

A description of Bawburgh and a piece of stone from the Church of SS Mary & Walstan were displayed in the tower, but whether or not they are still there is uncertain. In February 2003, Hamish Grant wrote from Rongai:

St Walstan's, Rongai, is alive and well … there are services in English and Kiswahili at least weekly. We are trying to scrape together some money to reroof it. I know nothing about the stone from the original St Walstan's though I do seem to recall seeing a picture of it.

LONDON

Victoria & Albert Museum

There is an intriguing **15th-century truncated glass panel** at the Victoria & Albert Museum in London, entitled 'Scene from a Saint's Life'. It measures 45.7 x 17.8cm and comes with no known provenance, although it was made in Norfolk. The panel shows a young boy, a purse at his girdle and a bag slung over his shoulder, about to leave a man and a woman, the woman having placed a hand on his shoulder. Ruby, blue and purple are used in the garments, and the hillside is painted on light green glass with the figures standing on an 'ears of barley' pedestal. This scene has never been safely identified, but the V&A favourably received a recent suggestion that it represents Walstan, Blida and Benedict.

In addition to the subject matter, i.e. perhaps that of the young Walstan leaving home, there is an obvious affinity between the son and his mother (St Blida?), who appears to have a specific emblem (something is tucked into her waist band, but St Blida's emblem is unknown). The 'ears of barley' pattern indicates Norwich work of around 1460-80 and is identical to that of the tiny fragment of glass incorporated into the window at Cawston which contains the name 'Blida'.

The scene was displayed in an exhibition at the Castle Museum in Norwich (1973), and the V&A has correspondence dating from the 1930s when suggestions for it were (a) Hannah bringing Samuel to Eli; and (b) a scene from the Life of St William of Norwich (as suggested by Christopher Woodforde who, however, added: '… I think that the panel represents a boyhood of some saint, but whether I am right about St William of Norwich is another matter. I mentioned the theory because it is Norwich glass.')

The case for SS Walstan and Blida, with Benedict, is therefore a possibility and these suggestions are put on record in the hope that the scene might, in time, be better identified.

REFERENCES:

Medieval Art in East Anglia 1300–1520 Edited by P Lasko and N J Morgan (Jarrolds, 1973)

'Scene from a Saint's Life' (Victoria & Albert Museum C351-1937)

SS Walstan & Blida Carol Twinch (NAHRG, 2001)

POSTCARDS, PAINTINGS AND HOLY PICTURES

Postcards of a Victorian print were sold during the 1940s and depicted St Walstan receiving the death message from an angel in front of Taverham Church.

On one copy of the postcard is written: 'From a rare old print kindly lent by Father Byrne, of Costessey'. However, both the print and the original are now lost – perhaps Father Byrne never got the print back from the printers!

Father Francis Byrne was the Catholic Priest at Costessey from 1910 until his death in 1924, and took part in the 1912 pilgrimage described in Picton's *A Great Gothic Fane*. He was the last Chaplain of Costessey Hall and the first Parish Priest of St Walstan's, Costessey.

Father Richard Wilson (of Costessey) confirms there is no trace of the print now either at St Walstan's Church or in the Presbytery. The style of the print is Victorian, and it is probable that it belonged to the Jerninghams of Costessey Hall and was either sold or given away when the hall was demolished in the 1920s.

Postcards showing the **hand-painted icon of St Walstan**, by Anna Dimascio, are sold in Bowthorpe, although the original icon was stolen from St Walstan's Cell in 1992. The painting was commissioned as part of the 1989 British Food & Farming Year (see also Bowthorpe in Norfolk Gazetteer). The late Anna Dimascio, a member of the Greek Orthodox Church, portrayed Walstan in Saxon dress.

Also on sale are **wooden, hand-carved figures** of St Walstan as he appears on the 1989 **concrete obelisk** (which stands beside the Prayer Cell in Bowthorpe). The carvings are six inches high, in primitive design, with scythe.

In the Church of SS Mary & Walstan at Bawburgh are two anonymous **paintings**, circa 1960, executed in the style of those panels of St Walstan at (a) Sparham, with two calves at foot, crowned, carrying scythe and sceptre, clothed in an ermined, gold cape; and (b) Barnham Broom, with scythe and wearing a green gown. Painting (b) has an additional cameo of Bawburgh village in the background.

The then incumbent, Rev John Watson, found both paintings in the vestry in 1983 and had them framed and hung in the church.

St Walstan appears on only one **Holy Picture**, long since out of print (pictured left). It was probably sold as a 'one off' at Walsingham in the 1940s or 1950s. Instead of the usual prayer on the reverse, it has a caption that reads:

Our Lady of Walsingham – Our Lady is depicted as the mother, cradling her Son in her arms. At her feet are the staff and scrip of a pilgrim, the former blossoming with the red roses of England. The other three important mediaeval shrines of Norfolk are represented by St Walstan of Bawburgh, the farmhand saint, kneeling on Our Lady's right: St William, the boy martyr of Norwich, standing on her left: and the Holy Rood of Bromholm shining above. From the Rood the stars of the Milky Way lead to Walsingham where they form a glory round Our Lady's head. The background is the ruined arch of Walsingham Priory.

The only clue as to the date or origin of the Holy Picture lies in its **artist**, **D Cowles**, though to date no specific information is forthcoming.

A Play

LIFE OF ST. WALSTON

specially written by

DOREEN IDLE

Thursday, June 12th, 1952

At 7.45 p.m.

At THE CHURCH FARM

BAWBURGH

by kind permission of Mr. and Mrs. Reynolds

Programmes, including Admission 1/6
Obtainable from the Vicar, 'Phone Hethersett 322 or
Mrs. Reynolds, Church Farm, Bawburgh,
'Phone Costessey 238.

Chapter 7

Prayers, Hymns, Poems and Plays

PRAYERS

(i) St Walstan's prayer at the hour of his death (*Nova Legenda Anglie*)

Oh hope and salvation of the believers,
O glory and rest of those who labour,
Good Jesus grant your servant this mercy,
That if a labourer should have any infirmity or other bodily disablement,
Or if compelled by necessity anyone should reverently visit me
With good will and in your Holy Name on behalf of brute animals,
May be not be denied your help and, I pray Lord,
May the brute animals be restored to health.

(ii) Prayer in the English Life

(which would probably have also appeared on the triptych from which it was copied in 1658)

You knight of Christ, Walston holy,
Your cry to hear thee meekly wee pray.
Shield us from mischeife, sorrow & folly,
Engendring and renewing from day to day.
Replenished with misery, Job doth truly say,
& bring us to health blessed with Jhesus right hand,
Him to love & know in everlasting land.

(iii) Prayer to St Walstan

Reputedly used by medieval pilgrims to the Shrine Chapel in Bawburgh. Quoted by Fr Husenbeth in *Walstan* (1859) but referenced only as 'the following [prayer] taken from the most ancient author of his Life'.

Oh, Holy Walstan,
Well do you deserve praise in the Church of God!
You may be compared to the apostles for your renunciation of temporal things;
You are like to the martyrs by penitential mortification of the flesh;
You are the companion of confessors for your almsgiving,
And pouring forth abundantly holy prayers.

Pray that we may so follow your steps in the way of truth and justice
And of perfect humility,
That we may be enabled to come with you to the kingdom of light and glory,
Through our Lord Jesus Christ,
Who reigns with the Father and the Holy Ghost
For endless ages of ages. Amen.

(iv) The St Walstan Year Prayer

Said for the first time during the Dedication Service of St Walstan's Cell, Bowthorpe, conducted by Rt Rev David Bentley, Bishop of Lynn, in January 1989. The 'St Walstan Year' was sponsored by Norwich Diocesan Board of Social Responsibility – Novicare – to coincide with British Food & Farming Year (1989).

Lord, our Father
Whose servant Walstan devoted his life to your service
And to the love of your land,
Bless our beloved county of Norfolk,
And grant us all a healing in our division,
A new understanding of your call to service,
And an unwavering determination
To live after the example of Jesus Christ, our Lord. Amen.

(v) Canon to the Holy Righteous Walstan of Taverham (which precedes the Nine Odes of the Orthodox Church) by Fr Elias Jones (1998)

O Righteous Walstan, thou didst leave they home
To labour for Christ in the fields of Taverham.
Through fasting, prayer and great humility
Thou hast gathered many for the harvest of Christ.
The Lord crowned thee as a saint
And bestowed upon thee the gift of miracles.
Pray then that our souls may be saved.
Canon to Our Righteous Father Amongst the Saints,
Walstan of Taverham.

HYMNS

(i) Hymn to Labouring Saints

Onward still the throng is moving
There Blandin's victory palm
Phocas brings his flowers immortal
Crispin joins the gladsome psalm;
There the scythe of gentle Walstan,
There the plough of Isidore
Faithful workers for the Master
Resting now for evermore.

In spite of exhaustive enquiries it has not been possible to find the original hymn from which this verse derives. Dr John Henderson at the Royal School of Church Music has searched all the known databases and checked the usual sources, but with no luck.

REFERENCES:

Memorials of Old Norfolk Astley H J Dukinfield (1908)

(ii) St Walstan's Hymn (Sussex Carol, English Traditional Melody) by Gary Simons (libretto: Sheila Upjohn)

A hymn composed for British Food & Farming Year 1989 was sung for the first time by the congregation of SS Mary and Walstan, at that year's Patronal Service.

In September 1996 a revised version of the hymn was sung at the Bishop of Norwich's Children's Pilgrimage at Bawburgh. Part of the last act of *Walstan*, a play by Sheila Upjohn, was performed by the Pilgrim Players, followed by a short address by the Bishop of Norwich, who led pilgrims to St Walstan's Well where they placed flowers around it.

How can we live our faith today
Who fear to follow Walstan's way
And turn with him from wealth and ease
Whatever God or fortune please?
>For dare we walk where Walstan trod
>To seek himself and find his God?

He saw through rank's unkind constraints
To freedom's portion sought by saints,
Enough to bless and heal the least
Of all creation, man and beast.
>And dare we walk where Walstan trod
>Beyond himself to seek his God?

He saw our Lord in human need;
And love so served to teach his creed
That all who knew him would perceive
The grace of faith and, so, believe.
>And dare we walk where Walstan trod
>To risk himself to share his God?

He worked God's land through rain and sun
To make of prayer and labour one,
And spoke the word of life through toil
That made his own the Kingdom's soil.
>And dare we walk where Walstan trod
>To give himself to witness God?

His was the trust to face known death
And yield in peace his harvest breath;
His was the life to Christ so given
That earth in him bore fruit of heaven.
>And dare we walk where Walstan trod
>To lose and find himself in God?

As oxen brought him whence he came
And spring were born to hear his name,
Where beasts and he, fulfilled, found rest,
Theirs but in sleep, his with the blest.
  So let us walk as Walstan trod
  And drawn with him, return to God.

POEMS

In 2000 Jenny Holmwood of Bowthorpe wrote *Walstan's Playground* as discussions continued about marking the Millennium by naming the old bridlepath that runs from Bowthorpe to Colney 'St Walstan's Way'.

Across grey roofs and skyline,
Lies the valley of the Yare.
Glossy waters beckon
Birds skim without a care.
Horses graze then gaze around
Trees shed copper leaves,
Through gaps in naked branches
The traffic idly weaves.

The structure of the pylon
Stands proudly strong and bold
To feed power to our houses
and keep us from the cold.
Beyond the rust and ochre
Lies a strip of lovat green,
And dots of homes and farmstead
Project against its screen.

The ancient path meanders
Wearing its modern face.
From Earlham down to Bawburgh
Where St Walstan used to pace.
The patron Saint of Farmers
Turned soil to sow the seed
To harvest hearts of wanting
And meet God in their need.

Echoes of the summer sing
As yellow hedges sway.
There have been a thousand summers
Since Walstan used to play.
St Michael and all angels
Stand in ruins on the hill.
A newer church now neighbours
But the spirit lives on still.

The archangel Michael
Champion fighter against sin,
Protector of Community
ferried Walstan's lifetime in.
So down throughout the ages
Plagues and wars took men away,
Though time's the biggest enemy
God is here to stay!

(Previously published in *Bawburgh News*, Issue 200)

PLAYS

Life of St Walston by Doreen Idle

Performed at Church Farm, Bawburgh on 12 June 1952. It was commissioned by the Revd Herbert Llewellyn Davies (Vicar of Bawburgh 1948-1954) who in 1951 organised the first pilgrimage to St Walstan's Well for twenty years and was instrumental in re-igniting the waning interest in St Walstan. (See page 130)

REFERENCES:

Bawburgh News (Vol 13-1530)

Chapter 8

Generic and Specific Emblems

ST WALSTAN

To denote royal connections, St Walstan's **generic** emblem is a **crown** and/or **sceptre**, both of which are shared by a large number of saints and could not by themselves be used to identify an individual saint's church iconography. It is the combination of either a crown or sceptre with the **specific** emblem, a **scythe** (sometimes with **two calves/oxen at foot**), which identifies St Walstan in pre-Reformation religious art, plus the likely location of East Anglia.

The pioneer of listing saints' emblems in the British Isles was the Revd F C Husenbeth, who published *Emblems of Saints* in 1850, drawing on previous work by contemporary antiquaries Dawson Turner, Mrs Jameson, the Revd Canon Rock and the Revd Richard Hart. He also used Butler's *Lives of the Saints*, which in turn relied on Capgrave's *Legends* and the NLA. In 1916 Maurice and Wilfred Drake published *Saints and their Emblems*, which was based on Husenbeth's work but considerably increased the number of listings from his original fifteen hundred to nearly five thousand.

Ecclesiastical artists of the pre-Reformation era used emblems as a way of denoting a particular saint, although it would not necessarily reflect the Life of that saint. As Helen Roeder explained in *Saints and Their Attributes*:

A beehive held by a bishop does not necessarily mean that he was an apiarist.

St Sidwell with scythe at (left) Wolborough, Devon and (right) Plymtree.

It is more likely that he was a man renowned for eloquence, like St Ambrose,
whose very name is ambrosial.

Roeder credits only SS Albert of Bergamo, Sidwell and Walstan with a scythe as their emblem.

In the ages before common literacy, the use of such emblems became both essential – and essentially universal – since they had to be recognised by pilgrims who travelled between continents visiting holy shrines, wells and chapels in foreign places. Such symbols transcended language and maintained the universality of the Christian Church (as did the use of Latin in church services and in those places where the written word is used in illustration, e.g. **S.** **Walstanus** at North Burlingham). Although there was the occasional borrowing of an emblem from one saint to another, the visual embodiment of saints was by and large universally portrayed. A figure with an arrow in his or her hand, for example, could be SS Cosmos and Damian, or St Giles, but if accompanied by a sceptre is more likely to be St Edmund (especially in East Anglia). St Stephen is associated with arrows, as are SS Ursula and Christina.

The **scythe** is employed by only a handful of saints, principally St Walstan and **St Sidwell** (or Sativola), an 11th-century saint local to Exeter. The two can, however, be distinguished from one another as Sidwell is a female saint, has no crown or sceptre, sometimes carries her head in her hands (as at Plymtree), and sometimes with a well nearby. (St Walstan's well only appears in post-Reformation narratives.) While St Walstan is likely to be identified in the East of England, St Sidwell is found principally in Devon, Cornwall and Somerset (although on some Devonshire screens Sidwell might be mistaken for her sister, Juthwara). A modern overlapping of this saintly territory appears to come at Eton College Chapel (Buckinghamshire) where Keyser gives St Sidwell as one of the figures on the north wall (an identification repeated by Mee in 1940 and confirmed by Duffy in 2001) and at Oxford All Souls. At Wolborough Church (Devonshire), however, Keyser gives 'Wulstan, Sidwell' on the north chantry screen, but this figure has not been substantiated or 'Wulstan' identified. Whereas Walstan was previously considered to be entirely 'local' to within a

20-mile radius of Norwich, so it might transpire that the cult of St Sidwell could have spread further east than is traditional. It is unlikely, though, that 'Wulstan' at Wolborough is St Walstan or that there could be any confusion between the two.

Identification of St Sidwell is so far confined to Laneast (Cornwall), and the Devonshire sites at Ashton, Exeter (cathedral and city church), Hennock, Holne, Kenn, Plymtree, South Sydenham and Wolborough. St Sidwell's Well is at Wick, Somerset. Sidwell's scythe has none of the sophistications of Walstan's and has no accompanying strickle.

In addition to the scythe, St Sidwell has one other factor in common with St Walstan. In Eamon Duffy's *The Voices of Morebath* can be found the story of St Sidwell's **silver shoe** (see also Introduction).

Others listed in Drake's *Saints and their Emblems* are SS Albert of Ogra (using a scythe to cut a stone), Guntilda, Nothburga, Valentius and Benedict. Husenbeth gives Walstan, Valentius and Sidwell (plus sickle and/or a well). Miriam Gill lists Sidwell, Urith of Chittlehampton, Valentius and Gunthilda.

There is no known instance of St Walstan's scythe being mistaken for a **Dance of Death** scythe although, by chance, two 15th-century Dance of Death panels accompany that of Walstan at Sparham (*qv*). Such extant portrayals of the Dance of Death are uncommon in East Anglia, although M R James (*Suffolk and Norfolk*) and Nelson both refer to 'a whole Dance of Death' once in St Andrew's, Norwich. The Dance of Death is an allegorical representation of death and often shows a skeleton leading various characters to their graves, sometimes holding a scythe. (See also Duffy's *Stripping of the Altars* for a discussion on the Dance of Death.)

Stained glass roundels depicting the seasons also show figures carrying or using scythes, but none raise any confusion with St Walstan. Christopher Woodforde (*The Norwich School of Glass-Painting in the Fifteenth Century*) cites examples such as that at Cassiobury Park (Hertfordshire) where scythes are employed by farmers and land workers illustrating haymaking.

At St Julian's (Norwich) the **wheatsheaf** held by the figure on the stem of the font (dated 1420) is attributed to St Walstan but is by no means a safe identification. The use of a wheatsheaf in religious art is puzzlingly sparse, given the immediate importance of grain in medieval life and the number of biblical references.

At North Burlingham (Norfolk, 1536), St Walstan gains a **purse**; the word **'opifer' (succourer)** or **'opifex' (worker, artisan)**; and in common with the other saints (Benedict, Edward the Confessor, Thomas of Canterbury, John the Baptist, Cecilia, Catherine, an unidentified figure, and Etheldreda) he is shown wearing **gold rings** on the second and fourth fingers of his right hand, and another on the thumb of his left hand that holds the scythe handle. In East Anglia the only significant use of the ring as a specific emblem would appear to be those worn by St Felix at Ranworth. It is likely that the rings at North Burlingham are a feature of art rather than having an intended significance except as a symbol of either pilgrimage or wealth. Rings were habitually included in medieval bequests, or gifts willed by pilgrims, as offerings for the repose of the donor's immortal soul.

The **purse** or **pouch** hanging from Walstan's waistband at North Burlingham has traditionally been assumed to be a purse, thereby denoting his charity to the poor. This supposition is all the more likely if the accompanying word on a panel in the hexagonal pedestal was originally 'opifer', to mean 'succourer' (literally 'helping').

It has also been suggested that the shell-like design to the purse is a **scallop**, similar to that worn by pilgrims to St James (the Great, of Compostela), or with reference to the seashell bed of St Felix the Martyr of Nola, thus depicting St Walstan as a pilgrim. The purse is a central feature of the painting and if interpreted as a pilgrim scallop it would be rare, as nowhere else is he represented as a pilgrim.

In his *Life of St Walstan*, however, Husenbeth calls it 'an elegant **scrip**' (a scrip being a beggar's, traveller's or pilgrim's wallet or satchel) and it is known that scallops were sewn on pilgrims' clothing or bags, so a connection might exist.

But if the word is 'opifex', and intended to mean 'maker', 'craftsman', or 'artisan', it is more likely to be a pouch for sand and/or grease, readily identified by a medieval craftsman as an important 'tool' for a farm labourer, namely the means to sharpen the blade of his scythe. The scythe itself shows a **detachable sharpener**, or **strickle**, at the base of the shaft and indicates that the designer knew something of the practical application of the use of a scythe. To the modern eye the accoutrement of a sharpener would be an unnecessary, and for the most part unnoticed, addition to the scythe. Indeed, a wooden sharpener for a metal blade at first seems impossible. However, no farm labourer who wielded a scythe could afford to be without his strickle and a pouch, or perhaps a horn, which contained the necessary ingredients of grease and fine sand to smear onto the wood, thereby creating the means to sharpen a metal blade.

In discussing the various agricultural tools employed in 15th-century glass, Christopher Woodforde observes:

> *Another interesting detail is the kind of scythe depicted in the various scenes. In the roundel from Cassiobury it resembles the modern form, but in all the Norwich examples the snath has a curious double end held by a pin or peg and, apparently, hinged. It is difficult to understand the purpose of this contraption, which was, perhaps, an East Anglian peculiarity.*

A strickle – which is Woodforde's 'curious double end' – is not an East Anglian peculiarity. (The 'snath' or 'snead' is the pole or shaft of the scythe made usually of willow, although the word can also mean 'to prune'.)

Using traditional reasoning, the **sceptre** (held by St Walstan at Foxearth, Sparham, Litcham and Ludham) has been accepted as a generic emblem in the same way as the crown, i.e. denoting royalty. However, the sceptre at Sparham is curiously clumsy for a symbol of royal wealth and is more likely to be an allegorical depiction of the strickle itself and not, as at first might appear, unsophisticated art. The head of the Sparham 'sceptre' has an ungainly, and deeply engrained, crisscross pattern that would take the grease and sand combination used to sharpen a metal blade and, while its entire shape is that of a sceptre, its head could be representational. The Ludham sceptre is barely a sceptre at all and accompanies one of the plainest of the pre-Reformation scythes. The Foxearth (Essex) sceptre has a lollipop shape over-painted with gold.

The **scythe** of St Walstan appears in a variety of pre-Reformation forms at Barnham Broom (the most perfect example of a strickle beyond doubt), Cavenham, Denton, Earl Stonham, Foxearth, Litcham, Ludham, North Burlingham, St Mary Magdalene (Norwich), Sparham and Earl Stonham. The form and design of the scythe is not always the same, but with the exception of Earl Stonham it is held upright, the blade shown behind or beside the head (although at Denton the blade curves behind the figure's right shoulder).

At St Mary Magdalene (Norwich) the artist has simply left it as a straight pole and a blade tied onto it with twine, reminiscent of the earliest form of scythe that employed the older sickle-like blade affixed to a straight-handle pole. Roy Brigden notes that the older and straighter form of shaft survived longer in northern Britain. The characteristic S-shaped shaft (not seen on any of St Walstan's scythes) evolved during the 12th century.

The Earl Stonham wood carving shows the scythe held differently to other images in that the blade is uppermost at his feet. The strickle is, therefore, upside down and would almost certainly have fallen out in practice. The shaft also appears to show a suggestion of a handle and is similar to that on the Denton panel painting.

Those images that have either the detachable sharpener, or strickle, at the base are at Barnham Broom, Denton (possibly with a strickle hook), Ludham, North Burlingham and Sparham, while those at Barnham Broom, Denton and Sparham illustrate the **'cradle'** type of scythe. This last had a loop, usually of hazel, attached to the upper part of the handle, or shaft, which cleared the crop out of the mower's path to leave a neat bundle for the followers to gather up. It is interesting to note that the cradle scythe was not used much in Britain until the 19th century (when it was used briefly to mow corn) and its depiction could indicate that the artists came from mainland Europe. An engraving by the Dutch artist Pieter Brueghel entitled 'Spring' (1565) is an almost perfect example of a cradle scythe in use. In addition it shows a worker at rest, the strickle out of its carrying position and two handles (one reminiscent of that at Denton) on the shaft. Quick and Buchele write:

> Probably the earliest example of a cradle scythe is that seen in an illuminated Psaltery of the 13th century. It showed a simple loop attached to the handle just above the blade similar to that illustrated by Brueghel in his classic engraving 'Spring' (1565). The purpose of the cradle attachment was to enable the reaper to deposit the bunch or gavel to the side of the swath in one action, clearing the way for the next stroke.

The cradle-type loop on the Walstan scythes is that described above, being too small for the later and much larger sail-like cradle.

At Denton the shaft has a pronounced **hook** a third of the way up its length, which is an impractical representation of a handle for the mower. The base of the quite short shaft shows a small, fine ring (described by Husenbeth as being similar to a modern shepherd's crook, but there is, however, no known example of such a combination tool). The ring is, in fact, the holder for the strickle.

The Sparham scythe has one of the most specific and detailed illustrations of a strickle and even has the rings into which the tapering tool fitted (as also seen at Denton).

Among the modern depictions of St Walstan is that intended for St Thomas' Church in Norwich, where he is seen holding the scythe blade in his right hand. (Kings of Norwich designed it in 1960 as a commemorative window but the donors changed their minds at the last minute and the work was never completed.)

Modern art historians are less familiar with the intricacies of the scythe and possibly would not recognise the need for a pouch or horn in which to carry the grease and sand; nor would they necessarily notice the particular design of the scythe (the blade being its most obvious characteristic). But the medieval artists who drew these figures would have been familiar with its practical application. Such attention to detail in the agricultural hand tools might point to their having been executed by either French or Flemish artists. The use of the scythe (and its sharpener) was more widespread in large parts of Europe and for longer than in Britain. As late as 1859, Husenbeth wrote of the 'antique wooden sharpener' that it 'may still be seen in use in some countries'.

Recent advances in dendrochronology raise a new dimension to interpretation of 13th-, 14th- and 15th-century depictions of saints on rood screens. The relatively new science of dating wood through study of tree ring growth has raised questions over the source of some rood screen paintings, as the wood on which they were painted is found to originate from countries beyond the British Isles. In March 2003 a study of the timbers used to build the roof of Salisbury Cathedral in the 13th century revealed that the timbers originated in Dublin. They were felled in the spring of 1222, two years after the Cathedral's foundation stone was laid.

So, if wood has been imported since at least the early 13th century, might the panels have been painted in their country of origin and not, as generally accepted, in the British Isles by itinerant artists? If so, this could account for the emphasis of detail in the practicalities of contemporary scythe technology, possibly of greater importance and significance outside Britain. The more common use of the scythe in many countries of origin of wood found in British churches could be a pointer in the discussion and academic investigation of the pace at which medieval rural societies devolved and evolved. At the very least it raises interesting questions about the paintings on the rood screens of East Anglia. It may be that we are looking at a trade of ready-made panels, bought and sold much as self-assembly furniture is today.

This is not a new theory, having been discussed by Edward Strange at the start of the 20th century in connection with the rood screen at Ranworth. He concludes that the Ranworth screen, at least, was English both in arrangement and detail and that the paintings were executed on the spot 'and not imported ready-made'.

If the lettering in the **flushwork panel** at Garboldisham is confirmed as containing a scythe blade (see Chapter 4), it is unique in the gazetteer. This panel is also interesting in that the letter has an accretion on the left hand side. Could this, perhaps, represent **ears of corn** or even a scythe sharpener? If this flushwork were eventually assigned to St Walstan it would be a significant addition to the list of attributions.

In modern times there is less need for strict adherence to the generally accepted pre-Reformation art emblems. New representations of long-established saints use unconventional means of identification and are, invariably, named by inscription. St Walstan has lost his scythe in some 20th-century icons, gaining a **spade** (Fritton, Gateley, Great Ryburgh); a **lantern** and **Bible** (St Laurence, Norwich); a **wheatsheaf** (Bledlow); a **cross** (Cowden and Kirby-le-Soken) and a **dog**, **staff** and **Bible** (Gaywood).

The oak pulpit carving at Gaywood is unique in its use of a **dog** as specific emblem and is interesting in so far as the 11th-century St Wendelin, a German Patron Saint of Shepherds and Peasants, is depicted with a staff and a dog at his feet. Like St Walstan, Wendelin was invoked on behalf of sick cattle.

Like the scythe, Walstan's **calf**, **calves** or **oxen** survive in post-Reformation religious art, especially in the 20th century. Only two pre-Reformation paintings contain the oxen – those at Barnham Broom, where there are two brown oxen at his feet, and Sparham, which has two cow-like animals at foot. In the 20th century there are two white oxen at Great Melton, and at Stanford Rivers can be seen a particularly good brown and white calf. Cowden also has two calves and the displaced sign for Easton College has Walstan's cart pulled by two oxen.

REFERENCES:

The Rood-Screen of Ranworth Church Edward F Strange (1902)

Agricultural Hand Tools Roy Brigden (1983)

The Grain Harvesters Graeme Quick & Wesley Buchele (1978)

English Church Dedications, with a Survey of Cornwall and Devon Nicholas Orme (1996)

www.sonic.net (and other dendrochronology websites)

ST BLIDA

Other than the panel at St Mary Magdalene (Norwich) there is nothing that would confirm or disprove an emblem as belonging to St Blida. However, on the panel she is shown crowned (to denote royalty), holding a **quill** in her right hand and clasping a **book** or **Bible** with her left hand.

Husenbeth says of the panel 'crowned, holding a book and palm' and is repeated by Drake.

In *English Votaries*, Bale refers to 'beanes in a serten number' in the verse:

If ye cannot slepe but slumber

Geve otes unto sayne Uncomber,

And beanes in a serten number,

Unto saynt Blase and saynt Blythe.

Presumably this poured scorn on a tradition or ritual to St Blythe which involved a number of beans, and links Blythe with St Blaise, Patron Saint of the woollen trade and a popular saint of Norwich. The tradition of offering oats to St Uncumber (otherwise Wilgefortis) is told in the *Oxford Dictionary of Saints* but to date no other clues have surfaced as to why anyone should offer beans to St Blida (or, for that matter, St Blaise).

CELEBRATION OF ST. WALSTAN 1989

DIOCESAN PILGRIMAGE TAVERHAM TO BAWBURGH

SUNDAY, 28th MAY, 1989
1.30 p.m.

MEET AT TAVERHAM 1 – 1.30 p.m.
CAR PARKING
RETURN BUS SERVICE 5 – 6 p.m.
FOR DRIVERS

EXHIBITION, STALLS, TEAS, AT BAWBURGH

HYMN SINGING EN ROUTE WITH TAVERHAM BAND

*OPEN AIR SERVICE ON THE MEADOW BY
THE RIVER AT BAWBURGH – 3.30 p.m.*

PREACHER: THE BISHOP OF NORWICH

British Food & Farming 1989

Regional Office:
80 St. Stephens Road,
Norwich, NR8 6RD.

Major sponsor and official insurer
The National Farmers Union Mutual Insurance Society Limited

Chapter 9

Miscellaneous Data

FEAST DATE

30 May is given in both the Latin and English Life and is generally accepted to be the date of St Walstan's death, and therefore his feast day.

Husenbeth, however, in his *Life of St Walstan* writes:

In some old English Calendars, the feast of St Walstan occurs on the 28th of December. It stands thus in the Catholic Almanac of 1687, also in the "Manual", Editions of 1706 and 1728; and likewise in the "Paradise of the Soul", 1720. But the day of the Saint's holy death, May 30th, has usually been considered his proper festival, and the venerable author of the Lives of the Saints, Alban Butler, gives his life of St Walstan on that day.

M R James gives the 'Manual' edition as 1708.

In his *History of Norfolk* Blomefield wrote '… he is said to die in 1016, on the third of the calends of June' which he took from the manuscripts of Thomas Tanner, to whom he dedicated his History.

The Roman Calendar was arranged around the Ides, Kalends and Nones. The Kalends of a month was the first of the month, but they counted backwards, beginning on what is now regarded as the previous month. Thus counting back from the third Kalends of June, we arrive at 30 May (Source: Rollason).

Other saints, including Felix Pope and Martyr, Hubert of Maastricht,

Ferdinand III and Joan of Arc, share 30 May (in one or other calendar), which often accounts for the omission of Walstan from shortened or edited lists. The Ramsgate Monks list 23 saints for 30 May in *The Book of Saints*.

The May and June dates can be significant in distinguishing Walstan of Bawburgh from Bishop Wulfstan, whose Feast Day is 19 January.

Just as we have no specific emblem for St Blida, there is no known record of her feast date.

PATRON SAINT OF FARM WORKERS AND AGRICULTURE

There is no record of how or when St Walstan was designated Patron Saint of Farm Workers, but it is clear from the writings of Bishop Bale that he was venerated as such at the time of the Reformation. In *English Votaries* (1546) Bale records:

> *[He] became after the maner of Priapus the God of their Feldes in Northfolke, and Gyde of their Harvestes, al Mowers and Sythe followers sekyng hym ones in the Yeare.*

In modern times his entry in the textbooks is as a Patron Saint of Farm Labourers, Husbandmen, and Stockmen. His association with agriculture has inspired church window dedications to those who worked on or were associated with the land and farming in their lifetimes. Farming families have chosen St Walstan in 20th-century stained glass (Stanford Rivers in Essex, Bledlow in Buckinghamshire and Great Melton in Norfolk among them).

There is no English Patron Saint of Farming and Agriculture, and few saints associated with farming in Britain. For the purpose of raising him above the ordinary farm worker, Walstan was 'promoted' to being of royal blood and a crown added to his specific emblems.

In 1989, St Walstan was named Patron Saint of British Food and Farming Year and on 28 May of that year a Diocesan Pilgrimage took place between Taverham and Bawburgh. (See page 150)

St Isidore (Madrid).

Farm animals occasionally make an appearance in church art but only two pre-Reformation paintings of St Walstan (at Barnham Broom and Sparham) include the oxen. There are sheep in the medieval glass at North Tuddenham (Norfolk), where one of the scenes in the life of St Margaret of Antioch shows her spinning as sheep feed beside her, and at Combs (Suffolk) which again illustrates the pastoral aspect of her cult. St Antony the Great's pig occurs, as does St Elois' horse, but with no claim to farming patronage.

In other European countries several examples of rural saints can be found, principally **St Isidore of Madrid** (1070-1130) whose Life is not dissimilar to that of St Walstan. His emblems include two oxen, a sickle or other hand tool, and a spring. St Isidore is honoured as Patron Saint of Farm Labourers in Spain, Canada and Mexico, and his feast date is 10 May. No iconography exists in East Anglia for St Isidore other than a road in Kesgrave's Grange Farm Estate, near Ipswich. The name 'St Isidores' was suggested by one of the owners of the land on which the Grange Farm homes were built in the 1990s.

Abbot Benedict (480-550) is Patron of Italian Farmers and author of the Rule that bears his name.

The *Oxford Dictionary of Saints* gives Phocas of Sinope as Patron of Agricultural Workers, but most versions of this 4th-century martyr name him Phocas the Gardener.

The American writer, Helen Roeder, names St Blida as Patron Saint of Mothers. However, she gives no reason or reference other than, in her introduction, she acknowledges Dr CH Talbot 'for information about the Anglo-Saxon saints venerated in England'.

Site of the old Shrine Chapel at Bawburgh. (Betty Martins)

Chapter 10

Wills, Bequests and Guilds

AS THE NUMBER of transcribed pre-Reformation wills increases it becomes clear that affection for and devotion to St Walstan extended beyond Norwich, Bawburgh and environs. They are also useful in establishing the joint dedication of Bawburgh Church as that of Our Lady (or St Mary) and St Walstan, and the existence of the Shrine Chapel. Blomefield records some of the earliest references, including that Beatrice le Barber released a messuage 'to the church of St Walstan at Bauburc, and to Sir Jefferey, vicar there' in about 1255. Helen Russell (1472) confirms the existence of St Walstan's Chapel 'in the same church', i.e. Bawburgh, while Robert Bernak (1433) refers to the grave of St Walstan in the church.

When we read of Robert Clarke (1503) leaving 2 shillings to the decoration of the image of St Walstan in Bawburgh Church, so that silver shoes can be made for him, it conjures a picture of what the interior of the church and chapel must once have looked like (although of course we have no proof that the testator's intent was carried out in full). Thomas Tyard's silver-gilt cross, with pearls on it, was probably among those items looted by the reformers in 1538 together with the silver adornments of St Walstan's image contributed over the years. Parishioners coming into such gilded places were awed and in reverence of what lay behind the wealth and power that created these beautiful things, i.e. the Church Authority, so far removed from their own dull circumstances. Which was, of course, the point – although it was ostensibly to praise and honour God, crave the intercession of his saints, and illustrate the extent of earthly glorification made of the best and most valuable temporal materials such as gold, silver and pearls.

The bequests that men and women make in their wills, instructions for pilgrimages to be carried out on their behalf, indulgences to hasten the passage of their soul through purgatory into heaven and donations to local guilds, bring us as near as we are likely to get to how it was in those times for individuals. Nothing else is as personal, or as immediate, as a last request, in most cases hoping to ensure earthly immortality. We may imagine William Gardiner, priest of the rood altar in St Edmund's monastery, carefully listing those possessions he wished to pass to the altar of 'St Walston' after his death. How grand this altar must have looked, draped with its cloth of silk. No doubt the family mourning Thomas Shemyng the Elder watched the painting of St Walston's image in Bawburgh Church, taking comfort from the continuity that it represented, not dreaming that in the lifetime of their children the Shrine Chapel would be destroyed and with it the image bearing the silver shoes and the pardon cross encrusted with pearls. Thomas Fuller of Mildenhall and John More of Gislingham were assured that, after death, their memory would linger for a short time and thereby gain a morsel of immortality for as long as the pilgrimages they requested were honoured.

The richness of these wills is by no means exhausted and it is not stretching incredulity to suppose that yet more immediacy for the cult of St Walstan will emerge as those like Peter Northeast (in Suffolk) continue their heroic transcriptions of these precious documents that speak to successive generations as nothing else can. They also remind us of what once was and how much we have lost.

What are we to make of John Waters' request to be buried near the window of 'St Walston' at Beccles, almost ten years after the Reformation? If nothing else, it is a further clue to the devotion in Suffolk to St Walstan and provides evidence of yet another lost icon.

References for early bequests to the Church of SS Mary & Walstan at Bawburgh, and to the shrine in St Walstan's Chapel, can be found in Blomefield's *Norfolk* in the Bawburgh entry. Sources for those not found in Blomefield, or which relate to Suffolk, are given appropriately where known. The help and advice of Peter Northeast in the matter of wills and their meaning was invaluable. The Glossary in *Wills of the Archdeaconry of Sudbury, 1439-1474: I*, edited by Peter Northeast, is particularly helpful when it comes to descriptions of items and practices mentioned in wills.

Note that 'Sir' is a shortened form of 'sire' and was a form of address given as a courtesy to a priest in mediaeval times. There were, also, various spellings of Bawburgh over the years, including Baber, Bawburc, Baauburg, Bayber, and others. Similarly, St Walstan appears as Walstone, Walston, etc. and the primary spelling has been used where it is known. A list of spelling deviations appears in *In Search of St Walstan*.

Abbreviations:
NRO: Norfolk Record Office
NCC: Norwich Consistory Court
PCC: Prerogative Court of Canterbury
PRO: Public Record Office
SROB: Suffolk Record Office – Bury St Edmunds
SROI: Suffolk Record Office – Ipswich

The old way of referring to Bury St Edmunds registers was by name; the PC500/2/... form has now superseded this.

ST WALSTAN
Suffolk and Norfolk

1255

Blomefield records:

> *[In about 1250] Beatrice, widow of* **John le Barber of Norwich**, *released to the church of St Walstan at Bauburc, and to Sir Jefferey, vicar there, a messuage, with the appurtenances in Bauburc, which Bartholomew, formerly vicar, purchased of her husband, in the presence of Anselin de Bauburc, and others.*

See Blomefield for other 13th century bequests concerning John and Beatrice le Barber.

1433

Robert Bernak (Vicar of Bawburgh), in his will dated 15 April, wanted to be buried in the chancel and left 3s 4d to the emendation of the grave (tumul) of St Walstan in the church.

(NCC 148 Surflete)

1457

William Gybbes (or Gybbys)

A clerk of Norwich, William Gybbes's will is dated 30 July 1457 and contains a large number of requests and bequests, including – 'I leave my black vestment to serve in the church of Bauburgh as long as it will last there'.

He was appointed Vicar of Bawburgh in 1439.

(NCC: 53 Brosyard)

1460

Thomas Esthawe, Vicar of Thornham (formerly of Bawburgh 1434-1439) bequeathed twenty shillings to rebuilding of the fabric of the chapel of St

Walstan at Bawburgh with a proviso that the work be completed within seven years of the benefactor's death.

(PRO:PCC Stokton PROB/11/4, 177-8)

This reference is provided by Robert Halliday, who points out that the will was missed from the microfilm of Stokton, and can only be seen at the PRO. He came across it in J F Williams' *Some Norfolk Churches and their Old Time Benefactors* (see NNAS bibliography), which read as though £10 had been bequeathed for the rebuilding of the north aisle of the church. The church was, however, that at Thornham and in fact the sum of twenty shillings was left 'to the fabric of the chapel of St Walstan of Bawburgh which is to be newly and skilfully edified on condition that within the next seven years after my death the work shall be sufficiently done'.

It is not clear if the chapel is being built or rebuilt, but 1460 would seem to be very late for any original building and is more likely repairs or extensions to an existing edifice. Twenty shillings, even in 1460, would not have built much of a chapel from scratch and previous bequests would indicate a following to St Walstan prior to 1460. What it does substantiate, however, is the existence of St Walstan's Chapel, though it is impossible to tell if the work was carried out within the specified seven years.

Peter Northeast comments:

I wonder what the original word interpreted as 'rebuilding' was? The usual word used was 'reparation' – both in English and Latin – which could refer to repairs (rebuilding) but often referred to new work, e.g. 'to the reparation of the new tower' – i.e. building. Unfortunately you can't tell whether he's having a totally new chapel built or rebuilding a pre-existent one.

1472

Helen Russell (widow) of Bawburgh (Babor) left 12 pence to the 'reparation' of St Walstan's Chapel in the same church.

(NRO:NCC/37/Paynot)

1485

Thomas Fuller of Mildenhall (Suffolk) wished for a pilgrim to go to seven places, including 'St Walstan'.

(SROB:IC500/2/11/Hervye 349)

1493

Dr Edmund Rightwis (or Rightwise), a Vicar of Bawburgh who died on 23 June 1493, was buried in the chancel and has a brass in the Church. In his will he invokes the protection of 'St Michael and St Walstan'. He was resident in the parish of St Michael at Plea in Norwich when he wrote his will.

(PCC 28 Doggett)

1493

John More of Gislingham (Suffolk) left instructions in his will for a pilgrimage to, among others, the shrine of 'saynte Walston'. Peter Northeast deciphered the will in 2002. (See also Chapter 5 for a full list of shrines.)

(SROB:IC500/2/11/Hervye 442)

1498

John Claryngton of Bawburgh – 12 pence to St Walstan's Guild.

(NRO:NCC 98 Multon)

1503

Robert Clarke (or Clerke) includes St Walstan in 'commendation of soul'; wants to be buried in the path before the porch and leaves 6s 8d to the leading of the porch [of Bawburgh]. He left an acre of bond land (with the licence of the lord) to the gild of St Walstan and 4 bushels of barley. He left 2 shillings to the 'painting' ['decoration'] of the image of St Walstan, 'that is, for silver shoes to be made for him' (transcribed by Peter Northeast).

(NRO:NCC 426 Popy)

1503

Sir William Gardiner, priest of the rood altar in the monastery of St Edmund (Suffolk) bequeathed '... to the altar of saynt Walston in the church of saynt Mary' a mass book and a pair of silver chalices, a vestment of blue sarsenet, a corporas case with a corporas in it, 2 altar cloths, an altar cloth of silk with a 'frontell' to the same, another cloth for the over-part of the altar of the suit before-named.

(SROB: Pye 129; IC500/2/4/129)

1505

Thomas Shemyng the Elder of Bawburgh bequeathed his soul (*inter al.*) to St Walstan, together with 10 shillings to paint the saint's image in Bawburgh Church and 12 pence to the saint's Guild.

(NRO:NCC 162 Ryxe)

1505/6

Thomas Tyard (or Tyerd) was Vicar of Bawburgh (from 1493 until his death) and in his will dated 20 November 1505 included St Walstan in the commendation of his soul. He left a 'processional' [book containing the music used in a church procession] and a copy of de Burgh's *Pupilla oculi* to Bawburgh Church, also:

> To the said church of Bawburgh a cross called a pardon crosse, silver and gilt, with pearls on it, in this condition, viz. that the parishioners or wardens of the town allow the vicar of the time to have custody and use of the cross at suitable

times, from each Easter up to the feast of All Saints following, and at other times as needed by and expedient for the vicar of the time, and after the feast of All Saints the cross to be in the custody of the parishioners or warden of the town.

Obviously Thomas Tyard was not confident as to the integrity of his fellow clergy, since he also left a pyx (a box, often silver or silver-gilt, i.e. silver covered with a thin layer of gold, in which the Blessed Sacrament – or reserved host – is retained) to be used for visiting the sick. Similar conditions of custody were imposed on the pyx, in order that it did not fall into private hands!

In addition:

… to the said church of Bawburgh a tunic for St Walstan, studded with silver pennies and other silver things attached to ('pertinen') the tunic, on the same condition as for the silver cross.

Thomas died on 1 January 1506 and his memorial brass can still be seen in the chancel at Bawburgh.

Peter Northeast points out that Thomas was something of an academic and that his 'BTh' would probably equate to a modern Bachelor of Divinity. He was also a man of some substance, holding land in several parishes.

(NCC 338 Ryxe)

1506

In Blomefield's 'Garboldesham' entry an account of the **John atte Cherche** bequest reads:

In 1506, John atte Cherche, of Garboldesham was buried in the churchyard of All-Hallows there, and gave 8 marks for an obit for a year, and 40s for a pilgrim to go to St James in Gales, in the next year of grace; and to a pilgrim to St Thomas of Canterbury 3s 4d, and to a pilgrim to St Mildred 12d, and to a pilgrim going to St Walstone's 6d.

The ruins of All Saints (or All Hallows) can still be seen just north of the existing church of St John the Baptist (see also Chapter 4 under Garboldisham).

1508

Nicholas Wade of Kenton (Suffolk) requested pilgrimages to be done by a priest; to Our Lady of Walsingham: to the good Rood of Beccles and to Bawburgh to St Walston, and to sing a mass at each.

(SROI:IC/AA2/3/21)

1508

Margaret Clarke (or Clerke) was probably the widow of Robert Clarke who died in 1503. She was definitely the widow of a Robert Clarke and they both referred to a son Robert. Although Margaret Clarke does not mention St Walstan she did leave a bequest to 'the gild', which would have been the one dedicated to St Walstan.

1526

John Billynge of Norton (Suffolk) requested pilgrimages to Our Lady of Walsingham and 'St Walston'.

(NRO:NCC 210 Briggs)

1526

John Kedell wanted to be buried in the churchyard of Our Blessed Lady and St Walstan in Bauburgh and left 2 latten candlesticks [latten is an alloy of tin and other metals], price 26s 8d, to the church.

(NCC 279 Attware)

1528

Sir Edmund Wethyr, LL.B, master of the charnel in Norwich, was buried in Holy Rood Chapel in the cathedral, and founded a priest to sing for him for three years, at his grave. He gave his Close of 3 acres in Baber to the vicar of Baber, and his successours, for a 'certayne', that is, that they should pray for his soul, and his friends' souls, every Sunday in the year, in the pulpit, and every Friday in the year remember him in his mass; and if any vicar neglects it, the alderman of the gild of 'our Lady and St Wolstone at Baber', and the brethren shall take the Close to sustain the gild, giving 4d. to the curate, and offering 1d. on his yerday for dirige and mass for evermore.

(NRO:NCC 156 Haywarde)

Blomefield gives the testator's Christian name as Thomas although he does elsewhere give Mr Edmund Wethir as Vicar of Bawburgh who resigned in 1518. The correct name is Edmund, spelt Wethyr or Wethir. The error is corrected by Northeast.

1530

William Rychers (or Rechers) – Vicar of Bawburgh (he has a brass in the church); he was appointed in 1518 but parson of Thelnetham (Suffolk) at his death. He made his will at Bawburgh on 2 January 1530/31, expressing his wish to be buried in Bawburgh chancel 'before the image of Our Lady where I myself have devised and chosen'.

He left 13s 4d to Bawburgh Church 'which I will that my executor shall dispose upon such things as shall be most necessary to the said church'.

He was also Rector of Bowthorpe in 1508 and died on 20 January 1531.

(NCC: 85 Alpe)

[In 1538 the Shrine Chapel at Bawburgh was destroyed, the Norwich Cathedral Priory abolished and Bawburgh Rectory transferred to the **Dean and Chapter of Norwich**. Part of that Reformation was the abolition of saints' shrines across the country and the compulsory cessation of pilgrimage and other 'idolatrous' practices.]

1547

John Waters the Elder of Beccles (Suffolk) desired to be buried 'in the churchyard, near the window of St Walston'.

The will, dated 28 May 1547, is the only evidence to date of the lost window of St Walstan in Beccles church.

(SROI: IC/AA2/15 fol 576)

ST BLIDA/BLYTHE/BLITHE
Norfolk

1522

Bequest from **Richard Fuller of Norwich**, tanner, who gave 10 shillings to the Church at Martham 'where St Blithe lyeth'.

(NRO:NCC 163 Alblaster)

THE GUILD OF ST WALSTAN
and
THE GUILD OF OUR LADY & ST WALSTAN
Bawburgh

Guilds (or Gilds) began in the 12th century as religious fraternities, kind of Medieval trades unions, which revolved round parish activities. Within their own communities they made provision for their members who fell on hard times and promoted the interests of their common trades. Larger guilds would often provide apprenticeships and their business was civic, and was not restricted to church matters, though religion was at the heart of all their functions, especially where a testator left a sum of money to provide for his funeral or memorial.

Testators left instructions for pilgrimages, or paid for a mass to be said for the repose of his or her soul, and officers of the guild would undertake to make the necessary arrangements with the priests. It is interesting that the Guild of St Walstan was still active to within ten years of the Reformation.

Guild activities would take place in a chapel attached to the church, or an aisle of the church, and it is likely that meetings of the Guild of St Walstan took place in the Shrine Chapel. There members discussed how funds would be spent, arranged funerals if necessary and oversaw a deceased's bequests or instructions (as per that of Sir Edmund Wethyr in 1528, where he leaves clear instructions to the alderman of the 'gild of our Lady and St Wolstone' about what should happen if his wishes are not carried out in full).

The guild members would also pray that the soul of the departed had a rapid passage through purgatory (to heaven) and were expected to attend funerals and commemorative masses during the year. No doubt they turned out in force to the funeral of Robert Clarke, as his will indicates that he was a prominent man in the community and left not only land to the 'gild of St Walstan' but money for decoration of St Walstan's image.

Thomas Tyard was fully aware of how potentially lax the priest's attitude might be towards his legacies, so he entrusted them instead to the parishioners who were likely to use them for the purposes intended. In such cases guild members were likely to take the lead in making sure bequests were fulfilled.

To date no surviving records or documentation relating to the Guild of St Walstan, or the Guild of Our Lady and St Walstan, have been discovered, but this is by no means unusual, since surviving evidence of any guild is rare. That it existed is, however, indisputable, since there are the 15th- and 16th-century will bequests as proof and, maybe, more to be discovered.

While the Guild at Bawburgh would inevitably have taken St Walstan as its patron, it would seem that he was not taken as patron of any other guild outside Bawburgh. Our Lady (or St Mary), of course, appears in guilds and church patronage under numerous names and guises. The joint dedication of Bawburgh Church accounts for the guild mentioned by Sir Edmund Wethyr. If there were guilds at Bawburgh other than that of St Walstan, no mention of it has yet come to light and Ken Farnhill thinks it unlikely:

> *My impression of saints like St Walstan is that, if they attracted guild dedications at all, they tended to be specific to an associated place – in St Walstan's case, Bawburgh, in St Withburga's case, Holkham and East Dereham. It's very unusual to see a parish which didn't have an explicit association with a local saint using him/her as a patron.*

Dr Virginia Bainbridge (*Gilds in the Medieval Countryside: Social & Religious Change in Cambridgeshire c1350-1558*) confirms that no gilds dedicated to St Walstan existed in Cambridgeshire and also suggests that there was just one local gild, that at Bawburgh.

Only one testator, Richard Fuller of Norwich, mentions 'St Blithe' and, to date, no evidence that a guild bearing her name existed either in Martham or elsewhere.

Ken Farnhill's Guilds (see bibliography) gives a sterling account of East Anglian guilds.

1498 – **John Claryngton** left 12 pence to St Walstan's Guild.

1503 – **Robert Clarke** left an acre of bond land to the Gild of St Walstan.

1505 – **Thomas Shemyng the Elder** bequeathed 12 pence to the Guild of St Walstan.

1508 – **Margaret Clarke** left a bequest to 'the gild', which would have been the Gild of St Walstan.

1528 – **Sir Edmund Wethyr** refers to 'the alderman of the gild of our Lady and St Walstone at Baber'.

BIBLIOGRAPHY

Publications or websites that pertain to individual churches or sites are listed separately in the Gazetteer chapters and do not appear in the bibliography unless they have a wider or general reference.

ADAIR, John *The Pilgrims' Way: Shrines and Saints in Britain and Ireland* (1978)

ARMSTRONG, Benjamin John *A Norfolk Diary* (1949)

ATTWATER, Donald *A Dictionary of Saints* (Burns & Oates, 1958)

ATTWATER, Donald *The Penguin Dictionary of Saints* (Penguin, 1965)

BAINBRIDGE, Virginia *Gilds in the Medieval Countryside: Social & Religious Change in Cambridgeshire c 1350-1558* (1996)

BALE, Bishop *The Acts of English Votaries* (1546)

BENEDICTINE Monks of St Augustine's Abbey, Ramsgate *The Book of Saints* (Adam & Charles Black, 1947)

BERTOUCH, Baroness de *The Life of Fr Ignatius, OSB, The Monk of Llanthony* (Methuen 1904)

BETJEMAN, John (Ed) *Collins Guide to English Parish Churches* (Collins, 1959)

BLOMEFIELD, Francis *History of Norfolk* (1805)

Supplement to Blomefield's *Norfolk* (Clement Ingleby of London, 1929)

BOND, Francis *Dedications & Patron Saints of English Churches, Ecclesiastical Symbolism, Saints and their Emblems* (Oxford University Press, 1914)

BRANDER, Michael *Soho for East Anglia* (1963)

BRYANT, T Hugh *The Churches of Norfolk* (1898-1915)

BUTLER, Rev Alban *The Lives of the Fathers, Martyrs, and Other Principal Saints* (D & J Sadlier, New York, 1853)

Butler's *Lives of the Saints* edited F C Husenbeth, DD, VG (1857-60)

Butler's *Lives of the Saints* edited by H Thurston & D Attwater (1956)

Butler's *Lives of the Saints* edited by Michael Walsh (Burns & Oats, 1991)

Butler's *Lives of Patron Saints* edited Michael Walsh (Burns & Oates, 1987)

BUTLER, N V Pierce *A Book of British Saints* (Faith Press Ltd, 1957)

CARPENTER, Edward *Thomas Tenison, Archbishop of Canterbury, His Life and Times* (SPCK, London, 1948)

CAUTLEY, H Munro *Norfolk Churches* (1949)

CAUTLEY, H Munro *Suffolk Churches and Their Treasures* (1954)

CHALLONER, Richard, Bishop *Britannia Sancta (The Lives of the most celebrated British, English, Scottish and Irish Saints who have flourished in these Islands)* 1745

COOPER, Trevor (Ed) *The Journal of William Dowsing, Iconoclasm in East Anglia during the English Civil War* (2001)

COX, Charles J *Country Churches of Norfolk Vols 1 & 2* (George Allen, 1911)

CRESSY, R F (a Benedictine Monk) *The Church History of Brittany* (1668)

DELEHAYE, Pere Hippolyte *The Legends of the Saints, An Introduction to Hagiography* Translated by V M Crawford (University of Notre Dame Press, 1961)

DIXON, G M *Folktales and Legends of Norfolk* (Minimax Books, 1980)

DIXON, Geoffrey M *Folktales and Legends of East Anglia* (1996)

DRAKE, Maurice and Wilfred *Saints and Their Emblems* (Warner Laurie, 1916)

DUFFY, Eamon *The Stripping of the Altars* (Yale University Press, 1992)

DUFFY, Eamon *The Voices of Morebath, Reformation and Rebellion in an English Village* (Yale University Press, 2001)

DUKINFIELD, Astley, H J *Memorials of Old Norfolk* (Bemrose & Son, 1908)

DUTT, William A *Norfolk* (Methuen, 1929)

DUTT, William A *Suffolk* (Methuen, 1927)

DUTT, William A *Highways and Byways in East Anglia* (Macmillan, 1923)

Excursions in the County of Norfolk, Vol II (1819)

FARMER, David Hugh *The Oxford Dictionary of Saints* (Oxford University Press, 4th Edition, 1997)

FARNHILL, Ken *Guilds and the Parish Community in Late Medieval East Anglia, c 1470-1550* (York, 2001)

GARDNER, Thomas *An Historical Account of Dunwich, Blithburgh, Southwold with remarks on some places contiguous thereto* (1754)

GREEN, E A *Saints and their Symbols* (Revised edition 1911)

HARROD, Wilhelmine and LINNELL, Rev C L S *Shell Guide to Norfolk* (1957)

HOLWECK, Rt Rev F G *A Biographical Dictionary of the Saints* (B Herder Book Co, 1924)

HORSTMAN, Carl *Nova Legenda Anglie* (Clarendon Press, 1901)

HUSENBETH, F C *The Life of St Walstan, Confessor* (Thomas Jones, 1859)

HUSENBETH, F C *Emblems of Saints by which they are distinguished in works of art* (Burns & Lambert, 1850)

JAMES, M R *Suffolk and Norfolk* (1930)

JAMESON, Anna Brownell Murphy (Mrs) *Sacred and Legendary Art* (1848 & various editions)

JEFFERY, P H *God's East Anglia* (1989)

JESSOPP, AUGUSTUS (DD) and JAMES, MONTAGUE RHODES (Litt.D) *The Life and Miracles of St William of Norwich by Thomas of Monmouth* 1896

JONES, Alison *The Wordsworth Dictionary of Saints* (1994)

JONES, Trefor *The English Saints* (Canterbury Press, 1999)

KEYSER, C E *List of Buildings in Great Britain having Mural and Other Painted Decorations* (1883)

LINNELL, Rev C L S *Norfolk Church Dedications* (St Anthony's Press, York, 1962)

MARSDEN, Walter *The Resting Places of East Anglia* (1987)

MEE, Arthur *Essex, Norfolk, Suffolk and other volumes of The King's England series* (Hodder & Stoughton, c 1940s)

MESSENT, Claude J W *The City Churches of Norwich* (H W Hunt, 1932)

MILBURN, R L P *Saints and Their Emblems in English Churches* (Oxford University Press, 1949)

MORRIS, Colin & ROBERTS, Peter (eds) *Pilgrimage: The English Experience from Becket to Bunyan* (2002)

MORTLOCK, D P *The Popular Guide to Suffolk Churches 3 vols* (Acorn Edition, 1988)

MORTLOCK, D and ROBERTS, C V *The Popular Guide to Norfolk Churches 3 vols* (Acorn Edition, 1985)

NELSON, Philip *Ancient Painted Glass in England, 1170-1500* (1913)

NORTHEAST, Peter (ed) *Wills of the Archdeaconry of Sudbury, 1439-1474: Part 1* (2001)

NOTT, Rt Revd Peter *Bishop Peter's Pilgrimage* (Canterbury Press, 1996)

PEVSNER, Nikolaus *The Buildings of England: North-West and South Norfolk* (& other volumes, circa 1960s)

PICTON J W *A Great Gothic Fane* (W T Pike & Co, 1913)

PORTER, Enid *The Folklore of East Anglia* (Batsford, 1974)

PYNSON, Richarde *The Kalendre of the newe Legende of Englande* (1516)

RAWCLIFFE, Carole *The Hospitals of Medieval Norwich* (1995)

ROEDER, Helen *Saints and their Attributes* (1956)

ROLLASON, David *Saints and Relics in Anglo-Saxon England* (1989)

RYE, Walter *Some Early English Inscriptions in Norfolk* (Various editions)

SHORTT, L M *Lives & Legends of English Saints* (Methuen, 1914)

SKIPPER, Keith *The Norfolk Connection* (1991)

SMITH, Alan *Sixty Saxon Saints* (Anglo Saxon Books, 1996)

SPENCER, Noel & KENT, Arnold *The Old Churches of Norwich* Revised by Alec Court (Jarrolds, 1990)

STANTON, Richard *A Menology of England and Wales* (1892)

TAYLOR, Richard *Index Monasticus, or The Abbeys and Other Monasteries, Alien Priories, Friaries ... formerly established in the Diocese of Norwich and the Ancient Kingdom of East Anglia* (1821)

THACKER, Alan & SHARPE, Richard (eds) *Local Saints and Local Churches in the Early Medieval West* (2002)

TOULSON, Shirley *East Anglia, Walking the Ley Lines and Ancient Tracks* (1981)

TWINCH, Carol *In Search of St Walstan: East Anglia's Enduring Legend* (1995)

TWINCH, Carol *Great Suffolk Stories* [pgs 185-187] (2003)

Victoria History of the Counties of Norfolk, Suffolk and Essex (circa 1906)

VINCE, John *Discovering Saints in Britain* (Shire Publications, 1990)

VORAGINE, Jacobus de *The Golden Legend* (Translated by William Granger Ryan, 1993)

WARNER, Peter *The Origins of Suffolk* (Manchester University Press, 1996)

WESTWOOD, Jennifer *Gothick Norfolk* (1989)

WILLIAMSON, Tom *The Origins of Norfolk* (1993)

WOODFORDE, Christopher *The Norwich School of Glass-Painting in the Fifteenth Century* (1950)

WYNKYNE de Worde *Nova Legenda Anglie* (1516)

Also:

MS Lambeth 935, Item 8 (The English Life of St Walstan)

Transcript of the English Life of St Walstan by Canon J C Morris on 6 December 1858 (Bishop's Library, Northampton)

Transcription of Morris MS by Fr F C Husenbeth on 30 December 1858 (with the old spelling modernised) (Bishop's Library, Northampton)

MS Bodleian Rawlinson G20

Bawburgh News editor Carol Twinch (Numbers 1-96)

Bawburgh News editor Betty Martins (Numbers 97 to date)

Gabriel Young, Clergyman and Local Historian (papers relating to history of Bawburgh and St Walstan) NRA MC 1681/1 (7825/Misc)

The Proceedings of the Norfolk & Norwich Archaeological Society:

Screen at North Burlingham John Gunn (Vol III, 1849)

The Shrines & Pilgrimages of the County of Norfolk Rev Richard Hart (Vol VI, 1864)

Bowthorpe Hall Rev Augustus Jessopp (Vol VIII, 1877)

Lives of St Walstan M R James (Vol XIX, 1917)

NNAS Excursion (to Bawburgh, 1928) (Vol XXIII, xxii-iii)

Medieval Glass Restored to Cawston Church Rev Christopher Woodforde (Vol XXV, 1935)

Some Norfolk Churches and their Old Time Benefactors J F Williams (Vol 37, pp 333-44, 1941)

A Prehistoric Site in the Yare Valley Henry de Caux (Vol XXVIII)

Saints on Norfolk Rood Screens and Pulpits W W Williamson (Vol XXXI, 1957)

Medieval Roodscreen in Norfolk and The Roodscreens of Norfolk Churches Dr Simon Cotton (Vol 40, 1987)

St Walstan of Bawburgh Robert Halliday (Vol XLIV, Part II, 2003)

Eastern Daily Press and ***Eastern Evening News:***
(EDP unless stated EEN)

Walks round Norwich: XIX Bawburgh (21 January 1905)
New Screen at Bawburgh Church (2 March 1905)
Bawburgh and its Church (Letters to the Editor, 12 July 1905)
Archaeology of the Drayton District: Bawburgh (8 May 1908)
A Norfolk Lourdes: Pilgrims at St Walstan's Well (8 September 1913)
Ninth Centenary of Norfolk Saint: The Story of St Walstan Walter Piper (6 June 1916)
Pilgrimage to Holy Well of St Walstan (7 August 1931)
Water in St Walstan's Well Unfit to Drink (16 July 1952)
Vicar Retains His Faith in Power of St Walstan's Well (17 July 1952)
Burial place of a Patron Saint ('Rambler' series, 1962)
A Norfolk Miscellany, St Walstan of Bawburgh S G Thicknesse (undated)
Neat and Tidy Again (2 February 1980)
Homes to Enclose Monuments (7 February 1980)
A Farming Saint Mavis Scarles (14 May 1983)
Giant Sculpture to Gentle Saint (25 June 1987)
How Norfolk will mark Farm Year (15 March 1988)
Ancient Well is Blessed (30 May 1988)
Saintly Patronage for Farming Year (14 January 1989)
New Role for Norfolk's Gentle Giant Charles Roberts (23 January 1989)
Icons watch over Anna as she paints the saints (17 February 1989)
Pilgrims Trace Saint's Journey (29 May 1989)
Mystery Hymn Writer Sought (29 October 1990)
A Saint for East Anglia ('Encore', 30 May 1995)
A Humble Farmworker is Honoured Charles Roberts (23 May 1995)
Bishop leads hundreds on the track of farmers' patron saint (9 September 1996)
Country Lane Gone For Ever (24 June 1999)
Person of the Millennium (EEN, 30 December 1999)
This Norfolk Lad (EEN 6 January 2000)
Do you remember …? St Walstan at Bowthorpe (EEN, 12 May 2003)
A memorial with a rich rural history Sally Simpson (EEN, 17 May 2003)
Curiosities – the farmworkers' saint (EDP 'Sunday', 7 February 2004)

East Anglian Magazine:
A Norfolk Holy Well Peter Fitzjohn (July 1934)
Bawburgh and St Walstan H de Caux (1948)
Saints of East Anglia N V Pierce Butler (May 1952)
The Pride of Norfolk Paul Johnson (July 1958)
St Walstan of Bawburgh, An Intriguing Local Saint of the Soil Ian Martin (July 1978)

Norfolk Archaeological and Historical Research Group:
St Walstan of Bawburgh Robert Halliday (No 13, 1994)
SS Walstan & Blida: A list of Norfolk Iconography & literary references Carol Twinch (No 42, 2001)

Miscellaneous:
Ipswich Journal (23 July 1763)
Norwich Mercury (16 July 1763)
Norwich Gazette (23 July & 22 August 1763)
The Gentleman's Magazine & Historical Chronicle (July-September 1763)
Norwich Mercury (29 May 1841)
Diocese of Northampton: A Pilgrimage to St Walstan's Well, at Babur, near Cossey 'Viator' (Weekly Register, 4 August 1860)
The Gentleman's Magazine Library, 1896 (Classified Collection, 1731-1868)
In Memoriam, Fr F C Husenbeth (Northampton Catholic Magazine, Vol 14, November 1872)
St Walstan and the Miraculous Well at Babur X Orr (Reprint from Norwich Mercury, November 1898)
Some Notes on the Rood Screens of Norfolk John T Varden (East Anglian Handbook 1890)
St Walstan of Bawburgh Norfolk and Norwich Notes and Queries (16 June 1900) [Reprinted EDP 'Sunday', 7 Feb 2004]
A Head Office Outing (The Norwich Union, Midsummer 1903)
St Walstan's Well (Fisher's Almanac and Annual, 1914)
Story of St Walstan Walter J Piper (Northamptonshire Diocesan Magazine 1915)
Some Norfolk Rood Screens Dom Cam Bede (Supplement to Blomefield's *Norfolk*, 1929)
A Forgotten Shrine in Norfolk Leslie Nicolson (Church Times, 1956)
At the Well of Saint Walstan Peter Fitzjohn (Church Observer No 116, 1957)
Notes for a discussion on Norfolk Folklore Frank Dale Sayer (NRO:L 398, 1972)
Bawburgh Conservation Area R I Maxwell, County Planning Officer (Norfolk County Council, January 1973)
St Walstan of Bawburgh B H Pettitt (Norfolk Fair, December 1978)
The Little Known Saint Carol Twinch (Town & Country, May 1979)
St Walstan R C Fiske (The Norfolk Ancestor, Vol 2, September 1981)
Farmworkers' Own Saint Carol Twinch (Farming News, June 1984)
Norfolk Fair Album Philip Hepworth (Norfolk Fair, undated)
A History of Church Farmhouse Geoffrey Kelly (privately published 1988)
Ministers and parish churches, the local church in transition, 950-1200 John Blair (ed) (Oxford University Committee for Archaeology, 1988)
Norfolk Village's Forgotten Saints (East Anglian Post, June 1988)
Food and Farming Year (Farming in East Anglia, April 1988)
Walstan of Bawburgh: Norfolk's Patron Saint of Agriculture Carol Twinch (Media Associates, 1989)
The Saint with a Scythe Miriam Gill (The Suffolk Institute of Archaeology & History, Vol XXXVIII Part 3, 1995)
Taking the Waters in Norfolk Mary Manning (Norfolk Industrial Archaeological Society, 1993)
St Walstan of Bawburgh Robert Halliday (Suffolk & Norfolk, February 1995)
National Monuments Record (English Heritage) Report TG 10NE9
The Search for a Saintly Legend (East Anglian Daily Times, 12 June 1995)
May – a Month of Feasts Edwina Kellock (Suffolk & Norfolk Life, 1996)

The Church of St Mary and St Walstan, Bawburgh Richard Butler-Stoney (Leaflet compiled for Church Tours in 1996)

Donkeys join in Pilgrimage Walk Jonathan Lumby (Norwich Diocesan News, October 1996)

Church Archaeology (Society for Church Archaeology, 1998)

Pilgrim's Progress Trefor Jones (Norfolk Journal, October 1998)

A Cell of Healing Eldred Willey (The Tablet, December 1991)

The Lambeth Life, St Walstan, and 'Blyborow' town Carol Twinch (The Poaching Priors of Blythburgh, ed Alan Mackley, the Blythburgh Society, 2001)

St Walstan of Bawburgh (Orthodox England, Vol 4, June 2001)

The Reredos at the Church of Laurence, Norwich Carol Twinch (Church Archaeology, 2003)

Medieval Paintings of St Walstan of Bawburgh and the Annunciation, Gisleham Anne Marshall (www.paintedchurch.org 2001)

New light on ancient documents (The Times, 27 February 2003)

Irish oak shakes beliefs about Salisbury's origins Simon de Bruxelles (The Times, 5 March 2003)

England, my England: At least I thought it was until they started poking about in the roof at Salisbury Cathedral Jonathan Meades (The Times, 8 March 2003)

Work in progress:

Decoding Flint Flushwork Devices on Suffolk and Norfolk Churches (working title) John Blatchly (to be published through the Suffolk Institute of Archaeology and History in late 2004 or early 2005)

Related Internet web sites:

Bawburgh News
www.bawburghnews.freeserve.co.uk

Patron Saints Index
www.catholic-forum.com/saints/indexsnt.htm

Saints and Angels – Catholic Online
www.catholic.org

Community of Aiden & Hilda
www.keeling.force9.co.uk

Calendar of Celtic and Old English Saints
www.nireland.com

Find a Church
www.findachurch.co.uk

Britannia Church: Christine Shrines of Britain
www.britannia.com/churches/shrines.html

INDEX